12
14
16
H J-
RNJCVM
Stratton
Hundred
Nulhavia deo
occi dens
Meridies
Septen trio
Oriens
Darkpoole
Nlouums lowe
to Kreade
Essorde of Ixerice
Arondell of Ixerice
Beedes hauen
Byrmarny
Barnardc Grenuile
house vyned
Hemire
Poffill
Stone
Barnard
Grenuile
Manme
to Manmy
Stratton
Dunacombe
to kempthorn
Fleombe
M Grenuile
Lee
to Copstone
Norton
Trestrame
Alkole
Ham
Launcelle
Stratton Sentinye
Kilkhamton
Gregory Chamyn
Ham
Alexcombe
Geo Grenuiles
Botesboxe
Anderdon
Speckett of
Deuon
Byre
12
14
16
18

This book belongs to

TIM DINGLE

For Rachael
for Rennie
with grateful thanks for your help
28 June 1980

The Book of Bude and Stratton 1980
has been published as a Limited
Edition of which
this is

Number **364**

A complete list of the
original subscribers is
printed at the back of the book

Dedication

For our respective fathers
Laurence Dudley Stamp
and
Montague Acland Bere
who both cared deeply for
the Bude-Stratton area.

THE BOOK OF BUDE AND STRATTON

FRONT COVER: 19th century views of ABOVE: Bude
Haven and BELOW: Stratton.

The sea lock and Chapel Rock today. (MM)

THE BOOK OF BUDE AND STRATTON

BY

RENNIE BERE &
BRYAN DUDLEY STAMP

BARRACUDA BOOKS LIMITED
BUCKINGHAM, ENGLAND
MCMLXXX

PUBLISHED BY BARRACUDA BOOKS LIMITED
BUCKINGHAM, ENGLAND
AND PRINTED BY
BOWMAN—ROCASTLE LIMITED
HERTFORD, ENGLAND

BOUND BY
BOOKBINDERS OF LONDON LIMITED
LONDON N5

JACKET PRINTED BY
CHENEY & SONS LIMITED
BANBURY, OXON

LITHOGRAPHY BY
SOUTH MIDLANDS LITHOPLATES LIMITED
LUTON, ENGLAND

DISPLAY SET IN BASKERVILLE
& TEXT SET IN 11/12PT BASKERVILLE BY
BRIAN ROBINSON
NORTH MARSTON, ENGLAND

ISBN 0 86023 055 4

Contents

Preface

Stratton has been for centuries an established market town but the beginnings of Bude as a watering place did not take shape until the early 19th century when sea bathing and fresh air from the oceans were considered by doctors as beneficial to health. Sir Thomas Acland, the then owner of Efford Manor, together with other great landowners and farmers of the neighbourhood fully realised the value of Bude shell-sand as an essential addition to the acid soil of this culm area, thus increasing the productivity of their lands. As a consequence, they decided to cut a canal to extend beyond Holsworthy on one branch and to Launceston on the other. The first quarter of the 19th century saw this project achieved, and tons of Bude sand, coal, machinery and other material were sent inland on the canal. All this, as well as provisions, came by sailing coasters from South Wales and Bristol. Trade grew, and Bude was on the map as a busy port.

The story of Bude's growth from being an outlying part of Stratton, with a few fishermen's cottages by the estuary, to the town we know today has been ably told by Rennie Bere and Bryan Dudley-Stamp in this absorbing book. They give the reader a vivid picture of the rich history of the area, whilst Rennie Bere, a great naturalist, discusses the interesting flora and fauna that abound—from the beautiful blue vernal squills found on the cliffs at Northcott Mouth to the buzzards, fulmars and ravens all to be seen close by.

The *Book of Bude and Stratton* will, I am sure, prove of absorbing interest to the 'natives' as well as the visitors, keen enough to read it whilst on holiday. It is a worthy addition to the growing number of Town Books of Cornwall so ably conceived and published by Clive Birch of Barracuda Books.

Foreword

I am happy to contribute a foreword to *The Book of Bude and Stratton,* and to think that my forebears have contributed to Bude and its neighbourhood. In particular, in the middle of the last century, my great, great grandfather, Sir Thomas, was deeply concerned for the harbour and did much to forward the construction of the canal. The bathing pool now frequently described as 'St Thomas's Pit' should be called 'Sir Thomas's', because he built it.

I am correspondingly sad that the former Acland property, like all the outlying Acland properties throughout the West, has had to be sold off so as to protect the two 'heartland' estates at Killerton and Holnicote, now given to the National Trust. I make no complaint. Everything is much better than in the 'good old days' of my great, great grandfather when it was normal for a farm worker's family to sleep, all sexes, in a single room; and abnormal for them to see anything other than bread and potatoes more than about three or four times a year.

I have happy memories of a summer holiday in Bude when I was in my late teens. I had a home made canoe in which I paddled my brothers and sister on the canal. And I well remember the righteous screams of rage from the bank when we offered bread to cygnets and closed our hands around their beaks when they trustingly accepted. At least we disproved the myth that a blow from a mother swan's wing can break a man's leg, or even a child's arm. It was also a great pleasure to stay in Efford Cottage with my mother and father during his successful by-election campaign in 1930.

I am happy to think that people in Bude are these days recognising themselves and each other as fellow members of a valuable community. This is being shown forth, not only in this book, but in other ways such as the opening of the Museum, the defence of the Downs, and in a general sense of social awareness. I am sure that all this makes the town a happier place for its thousands of visitors; and I offer all possible good wishes to those who are most closely involved in the work.

Richard Acland

Ole Bood

(From an incident at Waterloo Station.)

I went to London and Mother too,
Us zeed the Thames, the Tower, the Zoo,
Us did'n knaw then what more ver do,
So us traapsed away to Waterloo
    Ver home to Bood.

Our 'eads was addled with sights and sounds
Our 'earts was sick and tired of towns,
Our veet was achin' ver Zummerleaze Downs
    In dear ole Bood.

There was crowds of volks in the Bookin' 'all,
But of volks us knawed there wad'n a sawl
So I sticked me 'ead in a pigeon awl—
    'Two tickets ver Bood.'

I looked to Mother, 'er face was red,
'Hush Jan, be maazed? 'tis Bude,' 'er said,
But then the Clerk 'ee shawed 'ees 'ead,
    And—'Good Old Bood!'

All eager-like I says to 'un
'Be you from Bood, then, too, my son?'
''Ees, father, fey I be—no fun,
    I be from Bood.'

'And up ta ''Street'' where I was born
Could yer the sea and the coachman's horn,
And I tell 'ee London's cruel forlorn
    Beside ole Bood.'

'I wad'n a-born ta Bood' says I,
'But Bood I live and there I'll die,
'Tis a place where a-body can see the sky
    Is dear ole Bood.'

'And the streets by clayn and the houses too,
And the Station beateth Waterloo,
And even poor volks gets a voo,
    Home there to Bood.'

'So sonny, I'll see ole Bood to day,
And the Ceres sailin' in the Bay
And the beaudiful sunset o'er the zay,
And when I sees yer volks I'll say
    Yer love ta Bood.'

Jan Homer.

Introduction & Acknowledgements

This book is not a detailed parish history. It is a picture of the area, both within and without the town boundaries, as seen by the authors. They are conscious of the fact that they both live in Bude and may well have failed to do justice to Stratton. The two communities have always tended to keep themselves apart and still do so.

Today the north-eastern corner of Cornwall is dominated by Bude, the largest centre of population for almost 20 miles in any direction. The shops, banks, hotels and other business premises serve a wide area. Stratton—in spite of the magnificent church, the excellent modern hospital and the quaint old buildings beside the narrow streets—appears to the uninitiated to be little more than a poor relation while the neighbouring villages of Kilkhampton, Week St Mary, Launcells, Poundstock and Morwenstowe are on a smaller scale altogether, with Poughill a charming cross between an ancient village and a suburb.

It has not always been like this. All these places have ancient and honoured lineages denied to Bude. Stratton, moreover, is the parent town which looks upon its offspring at Bude as something of an upstart.

This book aims to describe how these places have changed and developed under the influence of their own particular histories; and to take a brief look at the life of the inhabitants in earlier centuries and the wildlife of a richly endowed area.

While writing this book and collecting the illustrations we have been helped by many people without whom it could not have been produced. Among those we wish to thank are: Lady Acland, Miss M. Venning, Mrs B. Worden, Mrs Budd, Mrs Rachael Dingle, John Thorn, Roy Thorn, Ron Spencer Thorn, Peter Cloke, George Cloke, Fred Dredge, Ken Cunningham (curator of the Town Museum), H. L. Douch (curator of the County Museum at Truro), the staff of the Bude branch of the Cornwall County Library, Edward Camilleri, C. Daniel, Michael Heard, Desmond Gregory, Ian Ballantyne, Leonard Burge, Dennis Jury, Peter Truscott, Andrew Jewell, Robert Hunt, Michael Smith, Mike Miller, John Beswick, John Stedwell, John Hough, Piers Brendon, Michael Bennett who typed the text and Maree Bere.

We are grateful also to Sir Richard Acland for his foreword, to Spencer Howlett for the preface and to our publisher Clive Birch.

ABOVE: Warbstow Bury, an Iron Age hill fort. (CW)
BELOW: The crags of Compass Point, looking north across Bude Bay. (RIC)

Paths to the Past

The Bude-Stratton area has been settled at least since the Bronze Age which in Cornwall is reckoned to have commenced in 1800 BC, that is nearly four thousand years ago. Barrows, or burial places of that period are still to be seen on Maer cliff and other hilltop sites in the neighbourhood, suggesting that man was then quite widely distributed and fairly active. Nothing remains, however, of any human presence before the New Stone Age though Mesolithic hunters and Neolithic settlers must have been present.

Both Kilkhampton and Stratton appear to have been settlements astride the old 'ridgeway' which ran from the Devon border to Padstow. 'These early ridgeways—most of which probably dated from Iron Age times—form the basis of a good deal of the secondary road system of modern Cornwall,' Prof W.G.V. Balchin in *Cornwall: Making of the English Landscape*.

Ridgeways took the line of least resistance, which meant following the watershed wherever possible, so you find the A39 (before the latest modern improvements) taking a line two miles inland at the head of the deep and narrow valleys running in from the sea. Close to this road are numerous tumuli, barrows, camps and castles, of which the best known is Kilkhampton Castle. Though this is the remains of a typical Norman castle it is reckoned to have been established on an earlier camp site. Almost immediately south of Kilkhampton lies Winswood Castle, another early encampment beside the ridgeway. Nearer Stratton there are camps at Herdbury (or Yardbury) in the Ivyleaf-Bush area and at Leigh which is just east of the town. The former is large and semi-circular and measures some 250 by 320 feet. The picture is of Kilkhampton, Stratton, Week St Mary and Warbstow, with ancient earthworks nearby, in a north-south line with Marhamchurch fitting neatly into the pattern.

In the centre of Stamford Hill, there is another encampment which dates before Roman times. Stratton is also sometimes said to be of Roman origin, the name deriving from a street laid down by the Romans, but this is unlikely. It is doubtful if the Romans spent more time than they had to in this part of Cornwall which they looked upon as barbaric. Though well established at Exeter they came to Cornwall as travellers and traders rather than as settlers. Stratton is likely to have been an early valley settlement guarded by the fort at Yardbury. Roman coins have been found near Bude, and the possibility of a small Roman settlement cannot be discarded altogether. South of Stratton, and still in the line of the A39 lies the Vil of Ponte, described in an indenture dated 1536 as 'otherwise called Hele', or Hele Bridge as it is known today. While Ponte, from *pons* (latin for bridge), suggests a Roman origin, the same syllable has the same meaning in Cornish and occurs in other place names further west.

The 5th century marked the beginning of the Dark Ages and the introduction of Christianity to Cornwall. There is little direct evidence of early Christian activity in the area except for a few holy wells, some of which survive, and the Cornish Cross in the grounds of Tonacombe Manor near Morwenstow which probably dates from the same period. Throughout the west of England the native inhabitants were then the Celtic British. Late in the 6th century the Saxon English landed in Kent. They reached Taunton and Exeter (*Isla Dumnoniorum* of the Romans) about 700 AD, cutting off the Celts of Devon and Cornwall from their fellows in Wales.

The Saxons continued to move west towards Cornwall, where the Celts made their last stand, keeping well to the north of Dartmoor and the deeper reaches of the Tamar. Battles raged back and forth across the shifting border between Saxon and Celt, the latter holding the western two thirds of Cornwall (originally *Cornewalas* which derives from the Saxon *Wealos*, ie: Welsh, meaning strangers) for another 200 years. There must have been a great deal of intermittent fighting around Stratton. As often happens, place names tell part of the story. Across the valley from Hele Bridge lay *Walesbrau* (again the word derives from *Wealos*) a fortress of the West Welsh on the site of the present Whalesborough Farm, indicating a boundary zone between the two warring populations. Today, Celtic names of towns and villages start around Poundstock; to its north, place names are of Saxon origin. Fighting continued until the reign of Athelstan (924-940) who finally established his supremacy throughout the country. It was Athelstan who fixed the River Tamar as the boundary between Devon and Cornwall, established an English style of administration in Cornwall and introduced the parochial system. Many of the parishes in the Bude-Stratton region can be traced from this period.

The Domesday survey of 1086 gives a firm picture of the area, and since most of the early manorial boundaries ran along streams it is possible to map them out. Among the more important manors in the district were: Kilkhampton (5,376 modern acres), Hilton and Launcells (each 1,576 acres), Stratton (1,536 acres), Pochehille or Poughill, Norton, Whitemot or Widemouth (each 768 acres), Whalesborough (560 acres), Marhamchurch and Cann Orchard (192 acres each) and Hele (48 acres). The large Kilkhampton manor was held by the King. The survey also shows that the area was well wooded, some of these Domesday woodlands still being identifiable. Among them are the Leigh Woods east of Stratton (20 acres), Scorsam Wood (30 acres), the Norton Woods (7 acres), Waadfast or Swannacott Woods near Week St Mary (15 acres) and Hele Wood (2 acres)—all these areas are given in Domesday acres, larger than modern acres but of uncertain extent. The old Hele Wood, now known as Whalesborough Wood, lies alongside the towpath by the Bude Canal.

These woods were classed as 'Lords' Woods' with cutting rights belonging to the tenants. In contrast to these woodland rights, the common people had no hunting rights whatsoever. Originally reserved for the Crown, hunting rights were sold to many of the larger landlords, particularly in the 13th century. There were deer parks at Launcells, Hornacott in North Tamerton and in the parish of Poundstock. But there were no royal hunting forests in the Stratton Hundred.

Saddle Rock and the Whale's Back. (RIC)

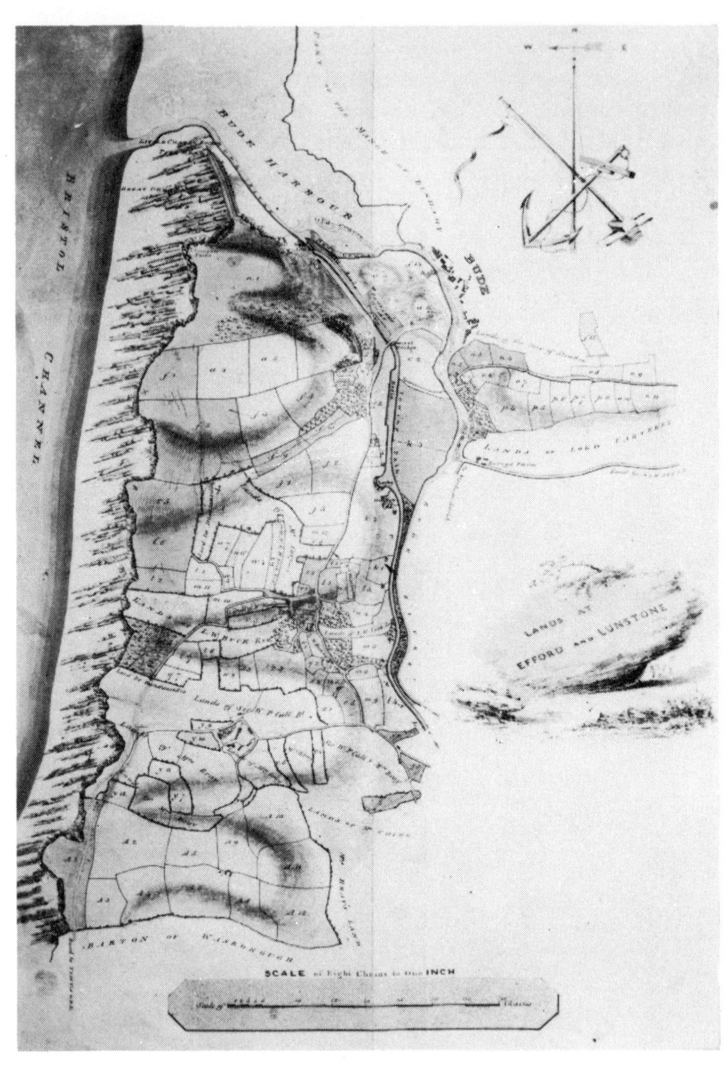

A map of the Efford and Lunstone lands c1820. (RST)

Stratton Hundred

Until the middle of the 19th century Bude was an outlying part of the parish of Stratton, a small town nestling around its church—'A market towne verie well served of all kynde of necessaries', according to John Wordens in 1584—together with the manors of Binhamy, Thurlibeer and Efford, or Ebbingford, near the sea where the River Neet could be forded at the ebb of the tide. Historically Efford would have been an appropriate name for Bude.

The origin of the name Bude is something of a mystery. Carew in the *Survey of Cornwall* (1602) uses 'Bude' for the haven and suggests that it derives from St Budoc or from *Boss,* or *Bod,* meaning a home or dwelling. Another possibility is the latin word *bed,* the part of a river which turned the wheel of a water-mill. There were two mills in the estuary, one at Hele and the other close to the sea at Efford. *The Dictionary of English Place Names* gives Bude as the name of the river as well as the haven and suggests that the name of the river may derive from Cornish *budr,* meaning dirty and referring to a stream with a muddy bottom. A more simple explanation could be that 'Bude' is a contraction of 'Bede' often used on early maps. There is, however, no known connection between the place and Venerable Bede, the 8th century scholar. Quite recently Leonard Burge, headmaster of the Bude Primary School, put forward what seems to be the most likely answer to this riddle. 'Bede' was once the term in general use for a 'holy man'. So it came about that mariners referred to the haven as 'Haven of the Holy Man' after the bede who occupied the chapel which once stood on Chapel Rock at the end of the breakwater and kept fires burning to guide ships into harbour.

The name Stratton is sometimes said to come from the latin *stratium,* 'the town on the street', presuming the existence of a Roman road. But there is no evidence of such a road, and the Romans are unlikely to have given the old ridgeway the status of a *strat*. It has been suggested that the name evolved from *Straetneat,* the road or way across the river. There is, however, a simpler explanation: that of *strat* (meaning street or road) and *ton* or *tun* (farm or manor) together meaning 'manor by the road.' As the Tree Inn, once the manor house, is on the road, this explanation makes good sense.

Stratton's roots go back a long way. It is mentioned in the will of Alfred the Great who died in 901, more than a century and a half before Domesday. There it is called *Straneaton Triconscire,* or 'Stratton in the shire of Trigg', 'shire' being the name then used in Cornwall for 'Hundred', the territorial division of land intermediate between county and vill. Later, Stratton was considered important enough to be given its own Hundred which, in a 14th century indenture, consisted of: Kylkamlonde (Kilkhampton), Marwinchurch (Marhamchurch), Boyton (Boyton), Jacobistowe (Jacobstowe), Wyteston (Whitstone), Stratone (Stratton), Poghaville (Poughill), Bruggerewal (Bridgerule), Wyke (Week St Mary), Launcels (Launcells), Tam'ton (North Tamerton) and Morwinstawe (Morwenstowe). Bridgerule is no longer administered as part of Cornwall but otherwise the Hundred remained more or less intact until the demise of the Stratton Rural District in the local government re-organisation of the 1970s. Poundstock was not part of the Stratton Hundred.

From an early date Stratton was the seat of justice for a wide area and continuity has been such that the Court Leet and a Court Baron were held annually in the Tree Inn until the 1900s; manorial rents were collected and the tenants given a free lunch and a clay pipe. Another mark of status was the fair, which received a charter from King John in 1207, and which was traditionally held on 19 May (St Andrew's Fair) and 10 December. There still is a regular cattle market at Stratton. Also, at least since mediaeval times, Stratton has been famous for its garlic. Not only did it grow wild, as it still does, but it was cultivated on a considerable scale, primarily as a cure for animal diseases. The remains of garlic cultivation are still to be found at Bowden, the 'Bude end' of Stratton.

The town of Stratton has never had a resident squire or Lord of the Manor. The running of the town was left largely to the churchwardens, and 'Eight General Inspectors, Stockwardens and Overseers of Accounts' commonly known as the 'Eight Men of Stratton', who were elected by a parish meeting. Their income came from rents, tolls levied upon fair-stall owners and from the sale of church ales, the cash being kept in a coffer deposited in the church tower. The Eight Men also administered a fund which still operates under the name of Blanchminster Charity, so called because Sir Ranulph Blanchminster of Binhamy left a small legacy to Stratton Church in the 14th century, and because the charity developed on what once had been Blanchminster lands.

The name Blanchminster Charity was not used until the 18th century. It was originally Norden's Charity named after William Norden who made one of the original benefactions in 1421. It then became the Stratton Town and Churchlands Charity which it remained for 200 years. Originally the charity was used for: service to the crown, including the equipping of soldiers, relief and maintenance of the poor of the parish of Stratton, and almost anything considered by the trustees to be of interest to the parishioners as a whole. In 1593, for example, the charity paid the expenses of three men who sued the Lord of the Manor, Sir Bernard Grenville of Stowe, for encroaching upon public fishing rights in the river near Poughill. In 1565, John Whytt was paid for 'castying the belle' while others that year were paid for 'wyne and good chere for the buschuppe ys servant'. Nicholas Rundell received 3½ yards of 'crease to make the poor Thomas a shroude', and in 1583 a poor man was helped who had lost a 'barke and all his goods at sea'. Distressed mariners and maimed soldiers were assisted at times and grants were made to leper-houses and for the defences of the county when Spanish invasion was threatened in 1588. Both Rodd's Bridge and Hele Bridge were rebuilt by the charity. In 1577 it helped rebuild the quay at Bude and pave the streets of Stratton, repeating this latter grant in the two subsequent centuries. Money was paid out for cleaning the streets in time of sickness and for 'watching one night at Efford when boats were seen approaching the shore (1596)', for killing foxes, building the school house, providing candlelight for choir boys, wine for the justices and once simply 'to make Mr Thomas Grenville drink'. The charity still distributes funds to the poor of the parish and provides educational grants.

Charitable trusts notwithstanding, it was the 17th century giant, Anthony Payne, who typified for many the true spirit of the people of Stratton—sturdy, steadfast and true:

> 'His sword was made to match his size,
> As Roundheads did remember,
> And when it swung t'was like the whirl
> Of windmills in September.'

Seven feet two inches tall at the age of 21 and of bulk and

weight that would have matched a mountain gorilla, Payne served the Grenville family at Stowe as a loyal retainer for over 40 years. There are many legends about him, the most famous being that his coffin was too large to be brought down the staircase of what is now the Tree Inn, where he had lived and died, and had to be lowered through a hole cut in the ceiling. Payne, whose portrait may be seen in the Truro museum, has given rise to a Cornish saying that anything of unusual length is 'as long as Tony Payne's foot'. Payne was buried in Stratton churchyard in 1691. Like the church of St Andrew—Hawker's 'tall Stratton tower'—he still watches over the place.

There may have been a church on this site as early as Saxon times. There certainly was a Norman church, relics of which were found during the restoration in the 19th century, and the existing font is Norman. The original rood screen was put up in 1534, King Henry VIII contributing towards the cost. Twenty years later, the Bishop of Exeter ordered its removal, which naturally upset the people of Stratton who pleaded for its retention. They offered to remove the figures of Christ, the Blessed Virgin Mary and St George, but to no avail. The Bishop sent men to Stratton who destroyed the screen. There is still a peal of eight bells which dates from this period (1558) and which is much admired by campanologists; the bells were recast in 1911.

'Stratton is a prettye towne' wrote Leland in 1600. It was also a town in which many folk seem to have enjoyed unusual longevity. In 1758, Elizabeth Cornish died at the age of 113 and her father before her, John Veal, survived until the extraordinary age of 114 years, 4 months and 15 days. He had not been ill for 40 years and ascribed his long life to the fact that he never drank spirituous liquors when young, and when old rose before 6.00 am both summer and winter and seldom ate meat. Not all the inhabitants were so healthy. In 1547, 150 people out of a population of 900 died of plague; and in 1729 smallpox carried off 42.

St James's Church at Kilkhampton is another typical Cornish church: except for the Norman doorway it is entirely late mediaeval. There is a fine wagon-roof and superbly carved bench-ends, most of which date from the 16th century, though one or two may have been carved 200 years earlier. The carvings include a series representing Christ's passion and others which are not sacred at all—a man with his performing bear, for example. Kilkhampton itself was a Saxon town, Kilcheton, a name which may derive from the Celtic *Killock* meaning a small cell or place of religious seclusion. From Tudor times until the present century it has been associated with the Grenville and, later, Thynne families.

Morwenstowe, the most northerly parish, is associated with the 19th century vicar, Rev Stephen Hawker. The church itself is one of the few in Cornwall which shows clear signs of a Norman origin in its interior, particularly in the north arcade where there are huge thick round piers with richly ornamented capitals and arches. Among the carvings are a hippopotamus' head and a pelican displaying the ancient belief that this bird fed its young with blood drawn from its own breast; this belief explains the mediaeval identification of the pelican with Christ's suffering on the cross. Thomas Kempthorne, who was vicar from 1559-1594 was also Lord of the Manor and built the fine old Tudor house which stands in the next coombe, south of the church. It is a good example of a small Elizabethan manor house, virtually unchanged since it was built. The stone fireplace in the hall is carved with the initials ER (Elizabeth Regina) and the date 1583.

The church at Poughill has an unusual dedication to St Olaf, a Danish saint, which suggests that there must have been an earlier church on the same site before the Conquest. The present building is largely 14th century. As at Kilkhampton there are fine bench-ends, one of which tells the story of Jonah being swallowed by the whale.

Another church with an interesting dedication is St Marwenna's at Marhamchurch with a remarkable mullioned window opening into an anchorite's cell. St Marwenna was one of the many daughters of the Welsh King Brychan who travelled to Cornwall during the 5th century. The place itself was originally Marona-Circa, the site of a much earlier settlement. Until about 1880 there was a mediaeval guild-house close to the lych-gate but it was removed to make way for an extension to the churchyard.

The church at Launcells is dedicated to St Andrew like the Stratton church to which it is a near neighbour. It is situated in a secluded wooded valley near St Swithin's holy well. The church has the same fine bench-ends as Kilkhampton and Poughill, believed to have been made in the same workshop, and beautiful glazed earthenware tiles on the chancel floor which came from Barnstaple in the 15th century. There is no village at Launcells, the needs of whose inhabitants in times past would have been met by Stratton; the parish still consists of scattered farms and homesteads. Another parish with its church in a wooded hollow is

Jacobstow but there a community is gathered around it.

Week St Mary once had the status of a borough and must, before the Conquest, have been a Saxon settlement on the Celtic frontier, the opposite of Whalesborough. Cole, the last Saxon owner, was replaced at the Conquest by a Norman, Baron Fitz Torold, who built a castle near the church, though few remains of this have ever been found.

'Our Lady of Week' has produced one of the great Cinderella stories of history. In the 15th century, the native Cornish moorland sheep were small and produced wool of poor quality which was exempted from the export duty, applied to protect the English wool industry. Merchants with continental connections made regular rounds of moorland farms to buy this wool. One, Richard Bunsby, saw there not only sheep but a young and pretty shepherd girl called Thomasine Bonaventura, of whom Richard Carew commented: 'I know not whether of event or descent so called.'

Bunsby took the girl to London to work in his household and married her a few years later when his first wife died. Bunsby died soon afterwards so Thomasine became a widow and an heiress. She married again, this time to a wealthy member of the Worshipful Company of Merchant Adventurers. He died and in 1497 she married Sir John Percyval who had been Sheriff of London in 1486 and became Lord Mayor the year after his marriage to Thomasine. The transformation from shepherd girl to Lord Mayor's wife was complete. Dame Percyval, as she had become, was widowed yet again in 1504. She returned to Week St Mary and devoted the rest of her life and fortune to good works in and around her home. She paid for the building of the church tower and founded a school or college which was described as 'a great comfort to all in the county for the sons of the best gentry in Devon and Cornwall were sent there.' Old College was abolished not long after Dame Thomasine's death (1520) under the Chantry Act, but parts of the building can still be seen in the village.

Of all the parishes which once looked to Stratton and now look to Bude, the quiet little village of Poundstock is the one with the most turbulent history. The parish church dedicated to St Neot (Abbot and cousin of Alfred the Great) was originally founded by missionaries from St Winvaloe's monastery in Brittany during the 6th century. Close to the church is a two-storeyed mediaeval guild-house, believed to be the oldest building of its type in Cornwall still in regular use.

The first recorded vicar was excommunicated in 1261. He was
a Bodrugan, one of the three families which dominated the parish
at the time; the others were Beville and Bloyou. About 20 years
afterwards a feud broke out between the vicars of Poundstock and
Morwenstowe over the endowment of their respective livings.
The predatory vicar of Morwenstowe, who complained that his
pay was insufficient, allied himself to the Bloyou family, came to
Poundstock with a gang of armed men and tried forcibly to
dispossess the vicar. They must have succeeded for a time as the
lawful incumbent appealed to the Archbishop of Canterbury who
came to Poundstock in person to re-instate him. In 1356, the
vicar, William de Penfoun, was murdered on the chancel steps of
his church as he finished saying mass. The background of this
affray is not known, nor are the names of the assassins whom
Bishop Grandisson of Exeter described as 'certain sattelites of
Satan, names unknown'.

The manor of Penfound is an ancient one, as is the house which
still stands with some pre-Norman features and a stream running
under the floor. It was originally occupied by Briend, the Saxon,
and later by the Penfound, or Penvoun, family. Sir William
Penfound was MP for Bodmin and bailiff of Stratton in the 15th
century. The Penfounds seem to have intermarried fairly
frequently with the Trebarfootes, although when a Penfound
daughter, Kate, tried to elope with John Trebarfoote, in 1650,
both the lovers were killed. Kate's father, Nicholas, had lost his
life only a few years previously while fighting under the Royalist
banner during the battle of Stamford Hill.

Almost exactly a century earlier, a national event occured
which affected the lives of countless individuals in every parish in
the land: the breaking of ecclesiastical ties with Rome.

Between the 12th and 16th centuries, monasteries were among
the larger landowners in many parts of Britain. But this was only
partly the situation in the Stratton Hundred where there were no
established monasteries—the small chantry at Week St Mary was
in a different category—and where monastic lands tended to be
scattered. The influence was strong, however, chiefly through
Launceston Priory, the largest religious house in Cornwall and
the well endowed abbey at Hartland—both belonged to the
Augustinian Monks. Launceston held the manor of Norton and
the piece of land known as the Manor of Sanctuary in Stratton.
The monks also had rights to the tithes of both Stratton and
Poughill. The Manor of Poughill belonged to Cleeve Abbey, the

ABOVE LEFT: Children in Backlane Hill, Stratton. (AJ)
CENTRE: Kilkhampton Church. (MM) RIGHT: Bench-ends inside the church; the one on the left shows the Grenville Arms: BELOW LEFT: The Judas bench-end in Launcells Church. (RH) RIGHT: Rodd's Bridge today: a bridge here was repaired by the Blanchminster Charity in the 16th century. (BM)

Cistercian house in Somerset, to which it had been given by Hubert de Burge (Minister of Henry III) in 1227. Tewkesbury Abbey in Gloucestershire held the advowson of Kilkhampton but not the manor which belonged to the Grenvilles. Hartland Abbey owned the Manor of Launcells, and Newenham Abbey in South Devon held the bailiwick of the whole Hundred obtained from William de Mohun in 1265.

Henry VIII's breach with Rome changed all this. Supreme jurisdiction in ecclesiastical matters passed from the Papacy to the Crown which, between 1529 and 1536 expropriated church lands and church wealth—the Dissolution of the Monasteries. But the King was soon involved in war with France, and this had to be paid for as had the rising costs of government—the economic situation of 1980 is not new. Church lands were gradually sold to the aristocracy and gentry, a process which increased the power of the landed classes vis-à-vis the Crown. Among those who benefitted were Sir Richard Grenville who had been a Steward of Bodmin Priory, securing the Manor of Norton, the advowson of Kilkhampton and other lands outside the Hundred. Sir John Chamond, another layman connected with monastic houses and chief Steward of Launceston, secured Launcells, owned by the monks of Hartland. His tomb is the only monument in the church. The Prideaux family of Padstow bought lands which had belonged to the chantry at Week St Mary while the Kempthornes and Waddons (of Morwenstowe) secured the Manor of Sanctuary. Other monastic lands and sources of wealth went elsewhere; and the few, such as Christopher Maunsell, of Launcells, who had remained faithful to the old religion and who were unable to pay the regulation fine, forfeited their goods and lands.

ABOVE: The tall Stratton Tower watches over the market town. (AJ) BELOW: The Bowden part of Stratton, centre of the garlic trade. (AJ)

ABOVE: Interior of Morwenstowe Church showing Norman pillars and decoration. (RST) CENTRE: Parliament buildings, the hamlet of Woodford in the parish of Morwenstowe. (AJ) BELOW: Outside the smithy in Marhamchurch. (AJ).

ABOVE: The Church of St Olaf at Poughill and BELOW:
Old cottages at Northcott Mouth. (BSHFE)

29

ABOVE: Launcells Church and Barton, once the home of Sir John Chamond. (RH) CENTRE: A lone figure enjoys the view of Widemouth Bay in 1877. Today the cliff is almost eroded back to the single cottage (the Salt House) which still stands. (RST) BELOW: Hawker's Morwenstowe; church and vicarage shortly after the vicarage was built. (A sketch by Sir Thomas Acland.)

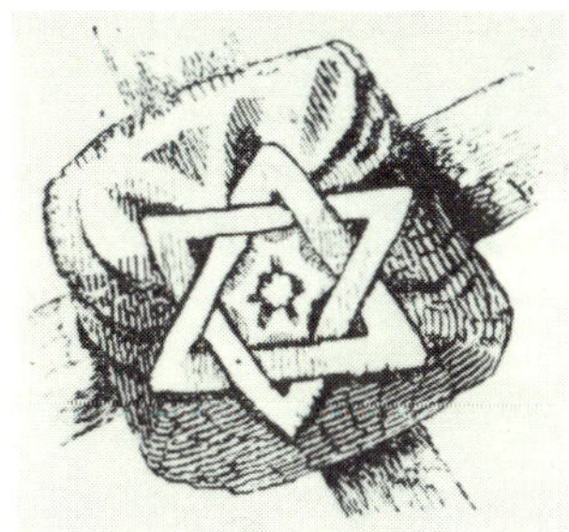 

ABOVE LEFT: The Shield of David on a boss in the chancel roof, Morwenstowe and RIGHT: on another, the Pentacle of Solomon. CENTRE: Efford Cottage and Chapel Rock. An 18th century watercolour, showing the Efford lime kilns and fish cellars. BELOW: View from Summerleaze beach towards the castle in the 19th century. Sea sand is being collected for use on inland fields. Beyond are St Michael's Church, Efford Cottage and the Falcon Hotel.

ABOVE: A 19th century engraving of Bude. BELOW: Efford Cottage before its reconstruction, and the old breakwater. A smack is outward bound. (A sketch by Sir Thomas Acland.)

The Battle of Stamford Hill

'In this place Ye Army of Ye rebells under ye command of Ye Earl of Stamford received a signal overthrow by ye valour of Sir Beville Grenville and ye Cornish Army on Tuesday ye 16th May, 1643.'

So reads the plaque placed at the centre of the Civil War battlefield of Stamford Hill, near Stratton, by the Bude-Stratton Old Cornwall Society in 1972. The plaque poses a query, for some accounts have it that the Earl of Stamford was not at the battle but laid up in Exeter with the gout. The historian of the Civil War, the Earl of Clarendon, clearly states however, that he was present—*Contemporary History of the Great Rebellion*, first published at Oxford in 1704. Whether Stamford was there or not, it is odd that the battle site should have been named after the general on the losing side. In fact, the naming seems fortuitous; Stamford Hill was in existence long before the event; the name appears in an entry of the Assize Roll of Cornwall for the year 1355.

The Battle of Stamford Hill was not one of the decisive battles of the war but it marked nevertheless an important phase in the struggle for dominance over the west of England between the Royalist and Parliamentary forces. The war had started in the summer of 1642. Later that year the Cornish Army, as it came to be known, was formed by Sir Bevil Grenville of Stowe, that famous house just north of Bude, and other Cornish Royalists including Colonel Trevanion and Sir Nicholas Slanning. Their first victory was achieved in January 1643, at Braddock Down near Bodmin. They were then joined by Sir Ralph Hopton of Withan, Somerset, an experienced general who had already fought in the Thirty Years War. It was he who marched northwards with Grenville to meet the Parliamentarians at Stratton. Something of the spirit of these stirring times is captured in this extract from R. S. Hawker's *The Gate Song of Stowe:*

Arise! and away! for the king and the law;
  Farewell to the couch and the pillow:
With spear in the rest, and with rein in the hand,
  Let us rush on the foe like a billow.

Call the hind from the plough, and the herd from the fold;
  Bid the wassailer cease from his revel;
And ride for old Stowe when the banner's unfurled
  For the cause of King Charles and Sir Bevil.

Travanion is up and Godolphin is nigh,
  And Harris of Hayne's o'er the river;
From Lundy to Looe, 'One and all!' is the cry,
  And 'the King and Sir Bevil for ever!'

Ay! by Tre, Pol and Pen, ye may know Cornishmen
  'Mid the names and the nobles of Devon;
But if truth to the King be a signal, why, then,
  Ye can find out the Grenville in heaven.

In early May the Royalists learned that the Earl of Stamford was advancing westwards and had reached Stratton; at all costs he must be prevented from moving deeper into Cornwall. By the evening of Sunday 14 May, Hopton and the Cornish Army had reached Week St Mary. In his narrative of the campaign, *Bellum Civile,* published in 1902 by the Somerset Record Society, Hopton writes:

'The Army stoode upon their guard all that night likewise still in very great want of provisions their owne stocks cruely affording a bisquett to a man, and the place so poore that it was not able to supply them in any proporcien.'

On the Monday they again marched north towards Stratton. Rather than attacking the town head on, the Army swung west towards Widemouth Bay, the result being that their left flank was secured by the sea. Again Hopton takes up the story:

'The next day, (Monday) by sunnsett they were advanced so far as Efford House being within the parish of Stratton about a mile from the Towne, and immediately with their forlorne hope beate in a party of the Enymies, and recovered the passe over the river att Efford-Mill which lay betweene them and the Enymies Camp.' The 'passe' referred to is Nanny Moore's Bridge and the ford close to it.

It is easy to see that if they were to be successful, the Cornish Army had first to establish a bridge-head across the River Neet. Once this had been achieved 'the Commanders of the Cornish

Army call'd a Councell of warr, where it was quicly resolv'd, notwithstanding the great visible disadvantage, that they must either force the Enymies Campe, while the most part of their horse and dragoones were from them, or unavoydably perish.' It had been discovered meanwhile that although the enemy had 13 cannon with them, their cavalry was still at Bodmin.

'And so in the beginning of that night a great part of the Army was drawen over that passe and placed in the Inclosures towards the Enemies Campe, (possibly the present Burn Gardens to the west of the Golf Course), and stoode all night at the armes ready to receive the Enemy which was expected to fall upon them.'

The rest of the army remained to the south of the river and camped that night on Efford Down. No doubt the officers slept at Efford House, then occupied by Mistress Mary Arundell, a staunch Royalist and a sister-in-law of Sir Nicholas Slanning, one of the troop commanders.

'About the break of day (16 May), muskett shott began to be exchanged between both parties. And within a while after the rest of the Cornish Army was drawen over likewise, and the foote being about 2,400, dyvided into fower parts, and the cannon being eight pieces equallie distributed to every part.' The Cornish then advanced in four columns up the approaches to Stamford Hill from the south.

'Mr John Digby with the horse and dragoones being then about 500, stoode upon a Sandy-Common (presumably the present Bude Golf Course) where there was a way leading up to the Enymies Campe, with order to charge anything that should come downe that way in a body, but else to stand firme in reserve'.

The fight which started at 5 am 'continued doubtfull', as Hopton puts it, 'with many countenances of various events till about three of the clock in the afternoone.' With their 'ammunicion' almost spent, the Cornish Army made one last pike and sword charge to take the top of the hill. Despite Sir Bevil Grenville being born to the ground in the shock, they were successful. The Parliamentary commander, Major General Chudleigh, was captured. 'Yet,' wrote Clarendon, 'he had failed in no part as a soldier, and had behaved himself with as much courage as a man could;' 1,700 of his troops were made prisoner. The Roundheads also lost 300 dead, all their cannon and baggage which included £5,000 of campaign funds. A query must remain over the Earl of Stamford. Hopton, the eye-witness, makes no mention of him but Clarendon clearly believed that he had been

there as this extract from *The History of the Great Rebellion* (OUP
and Folio Society edition, 1967) shows:
'But the enemy no sooner understood the loss of their Major-
General but their hearts failed them; and being so resolutely
pressed, and their ground lost—upon the security and advantage
whereof they wholly depended—some of them threw down their
arms and others fled, dispersing themselves and every man
shifting for himself. Their General, the Earl of Stamford, gave the
example, who—having stood at a safe distance all the time of the
battle, environed with all the horse, which in small parties
(though it is true their whole number was not above six or seven
score) might have done great mischief to the several parties of
foot, who with so much difficulty scaled the steep hill—as soon as
he saw the day lost (and some said sooner) made all imaginable
haste to Exeter, to prepare them for the condition they were
shortly to expect.'

More important is the fact that, although outnumbered by
more than two to one, the Cornish Army by their sheer courage
won the day.

After victory prayers had been said, the Army spent the night
and the next day, Wednesday, in Stratton. On the Thursday they
marched off southwards to Launceston leaving behind Sir Bevil
Grenville to guard the prisoners and look after the captured
booty.

What of the battle's aftermath? Tradition has it that the dead
were buried in a mass grave on Maer Down, just above Crooklets
beach. This may be so as many cannon balls have been found
nearby; but if it is, it means that at least one Anthony Payne story
is fiction. When the giant was burying the dead, one of the
supposed corpses suddenly came round and began to plead for his
life:

'I be not dead, Mr Payne, I asn't done living yet.'

'I won't hurry thee, thou cans't die at thy leisure' Payne
replied carrying the man to his (Payne's) home in Stratton to be
nursed back to health by his wife.

Inspired by his success, Hopton and Grenville and the Cornish
Army advanced eastwards across the Tamar to be victorious yet
again, on 5 July, at Lansdowne, near Bath, where Grenville was
killed. Sir Bevil, gallant as ever, was struck on the head with a
pole-axe while leading his men into battle. Payne was present as
was Sir Bevil's son John, who later became 1st Earl of Bath.
Payne, so the story goes, mounted the boy on his father's charger,

rallied their dismayed followers and finally won the day. The Cornishmen had suffered fearful casualties but, despite the death of their beloved leader, gained a further victory at Roundway Down, near Devizes, a fortnight later. The saga of this successful Cornish Army ended with the seige of Bristol in August 1643; it was then disbanded.

It was left to Anthony Payne to bring his master's body back to Stowe from the Lansdowne battlefield. Hawker quotes him as writing to Lady Grenville:

'I am coming down with the mournfullest load that ever a poor servant did bear, to bring the great heart that is cold to Kilkhampton vault. Oh, my lady, how shall I brook your weeping face? But I will be trothful to the living and to the dead.

These words, honoured Madam, from thy saddest truest servant, Anthony Payne.'

What happened to the other participants in the battle? Major General Chudleigh was so impressed by the devotion of the Royalist army that he changed sides and fought for the King. Sir Ralph Hopton was created Lord Hopton of Stratton on 4 September, 1643, after the summer's campaign. He ended his days sadly in exile and died in Bruges in 1652, when the title became extinct. At the Restoration, Charles II bestowed the title on Sir John Berkeley, a staunch Royalist who had also fought at Stamford Hill. He is famous for developing his farm in the centre of London into Berkeley Square, with Stratton Street nearby. Thus he gave Stratton, and indirectly the battle, a permanent memorial in the nation's capital.

Those who would capture the feeling of this momentous day of long ago can still visit the battlefield or gaze pensively at the many 'Royal Coats of Arms' which decorate several local churches. These were given by Charles II as a tribute to those who had perished after being loyal to his father's cause. These silent monuments bear witness to the day when Stratton stood upon the national stage and the outnumbered Cornish Army won its first great victory for the Royalist cause in the west.

ABOVE: Anthony Payne (c1612-1691), giant retainer of Sir Bevil Grenville. A painting by Sir Godfrey Kneller in the Cornwall County Museum. (RIC) LEFT: His flagon. CENTRE: Sir Ralph Hopton, Civil War diarist and victorious General at the Battle of Stamford Hill. BELOW: Sir Bevil Grenville of Stowe. (PBT)

Lords and Manors

The Domesday manor of Stratton was held by Robert, Count of Mortain. In 1184 it seems to have been divided into two separate manors, Binhamy and Efford, the former of which descended upon the crusading family of Blanchminster (de Albo Monasterio) which survived for four or five generations. The family name is commemorated by the Blanchminster Charity (described earlier) and by the effigy in Stratton Church of Knight Templar, Sir Ranulph de Blanchminster, who is said to have gone on a crusade to the Holy Land with Prince Edward, later Edward I, in 1270 and to have been slain there. A later Blanchminster built the castle at Binhamy about the year 1335; the remains of this can still be seen a short distance west of the A39 road. Not long afterwards, Binhamy, together with some residual part of the Stratton manor itself, was conveyed to the Tresilians and then to the Coleshulls, another ancient Cornish family. On the demise of the Coleshulls, it became the property of one John Danvers. In 1576, both Stratton and Binhamy were purchased by Sir Richard Grenville who was to perish fifteen years later after his famous battle on the *Revenge*. These manors were held intact by the Grenville and Thynne families for nearly 350 years, until 18 June 1918, when they were auctioned and sold up following the death of Lt Col Algernon C. Thynne, killed on active service in Palestine during World War I. There is a fine memorial in Kilkhampton church.

The earliest known owners of Efford Manor, the other half of the original Stratton Manor, were the Heriz family, followed by the Waumfords and Durants. In 1410 it was acquired through marriage by the Arundels of Trerice, near Newquay. On the death of the last of the line of Arundel or Trerice, in 1768, Efford passed to the Wentworths, of Wentworth Castle in Yorkshire, the family of the Earl of Strafford. When they died out in 1802 it came to Sir Thomas Dyke Acland, 10th baronet, of Killerton, near Exeter. This happened because the 2nd Baron Arundel of Trerice had married Margaret, only daughter of Sir John Acland,

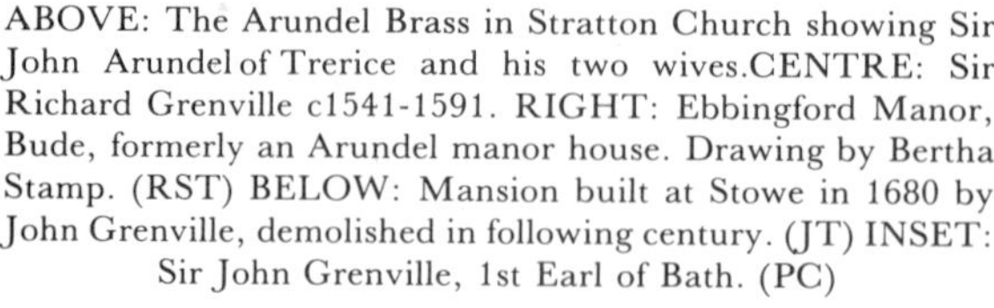

ABOVE: The Arundel Brass in Stratton Church showing Sir John Arundel of Trerice and his two wives. CENTRE: Sir Richard Grenville c1541-1591. RIGHT: Ebbingford Manor, Bude, formerly an Arundel manor house. Drawing by Bertha Stamp. (RST) BELOW: Mansion built at Stowe in 1680 by John Grenville, demolished in following century. (JT) INSET: Sir John Grenville, 1st Earl of Bath. (PC)

3rd baronet, c1675. The 4th and last Baron Arundel was thus a grandson of Margaret Acland.

At the Conquest, the manor of Poughill, later to be known as Broomhill (now a farmhouse), had been granted to William Capra under the overlordship of the Count of Mortain, and eventually became the property of Cleeve Abbey. After Dissolution and seizure by the Crown it was sold (1607) to one George Saltern from whom it descended to many different families including Kingdons, Hockins and Brendons, all of whom are still with us. The smaller estates of Maer and Flexbury, part of the original manor, were sold off separately.

The most interesting point of all this is that almost the whole of the built-up urban area of Bude and Stratton may properly be said to have been owned for the past 400 years, and well into the present century, by only two sets of landlords—the Arundels and later the Aclands on one side of the river, the Grenvilles and their kinsmen the Thynnes on the other. There were only two other landowners of consequence: the Blanchminster Charity and the Manor of Sanctuary in Stratton. The Manor of Sanctuary, a small parcel of land near Stratton church was once the property of Launceston Priory, was annexed to the Duchy of Cornwall after Dissolution, the Duke of Cornwall still being patron of the living of Stratton.

The Grenvilles and Arundels of Trerice seem always to have been on good terms, particularly during the 16th and 17th centuries. The families had intermarried and co-operated in various undertakings from defence of the realm to building a salt-water mill across the mouth of the River Neet in the year 1589. Since purchasing Binhamy Manor in 1576 Sir Richard Grenville had owned the river bank on one side and Lady Gertrude Arundel (née Dennis) the other. Bude Bridge was built—now known as Nanny Moore's after the 19th century 'dipper' who lived in a nearby cottage— and Efford Mill established. This was worked by the flow of the tide, sea-water being trapped in a mill-pond and released when the tide went out. Many such mills were built in the west country during the 15th and 16th centuries, though only five have been recorded on the north Cornish coast. The old mill cottage still stands; and as it is now used as a bakery and bears the appropriate name of 'Leven', association with the grinding of flour is very properly retained. Built into a wall of the cottage is a granite block inscribed, 'AJA 1589' (Anne and John Arundel) and showing the arms of the Dennis family. Lady

Arundel who built the mill was the second wife of Sir John Arundel (1548-1580) whose father, another Sir John, lies buried in Stratton church where a fine brass honours his memory. Widely known as 'Jack of Tilbury' this splendid man was twice Sheriff of Cornwall, Vice-Admiral of the West and Esquire of the body of Henry VIII.

The two families had much in common. Both were Norman in origin and came to England with William the Conquerer. Both were staunchly loyal to the Crown and were rewarded with peerages after the Civil War. Both became extinct during the 18th century. Both families built notable houses: Trerice, now property of the National Trust, near Newquay, in 1572; and Stowe above the Coombe Valley. The latter, a large rambling building, half castle and half dwelling house, was considered insufficiently grand by John Grenville, first Earl of Bath, and was demolished in 1662 to be replaced by a great red brick mansion which has been described as 'bedizened with every monstrosity of bad taste' and, by William Borlase as 'by far the noblest in the West of England, but not a tree to shelter it.' In 1739 it was pulled down by its then owner, the Earl's daughter, Grace Countess Grenville. 'An old man,' wrote Charles Kingsley in *Westward Ho!* 'who had seen as a boy the foundation of the new house laid, lived to see it pulled down again and the very bricks and timber sold upon the spot.' Since then the stables have become a farmhouse (the present Stowe Barton), the tennis court a sheepcote, the great quadrangle a rick yard.

By this time, the last of the Grenvilles in the direct male line, William Henry, 3rd Earl of Bath, had died. The properties then passed to a kinsman, Henry Thynne, Lord Carteret, and eventually (1849) to Lord John Thynne, nephew of the last Lord Carteret and the first true Lord of the Manor in the new line. Meanwhile the old Grenville lands had been managed by absentee landlords but soon (1862) the Thynnes built the relatively modest Penstowe (Upper Stowe) and came to live in the area. Rev Lord John Thynne (1798-1881), being patron of the living of Kilkhampton, instituted as vicar his youngest son, Arthur Christopher, who occupied Penstowe and let the rectory. The Thynnes reigned at Kilkhampton for 100 years, until Mrs Constance Thynne died at the age of 90 in 1961. What was left of the estate was then sold: Penstowe is now a holiday village.

The Thynnes followed a Grenville tradition by taking an interest in the port of Bude. As early as 1780 they leased off land for the building of the Bewd Inn, or Bude Hotel as it became known, built on the site of the present Lloyds Bank. At about this time two warehouses were built along the Strand, one on the site of Julia's Place, the other on that of the Strand Hotel. After the arrival of the railway in 1898, the Thynnes played an active part in the development of Bude. Opening the Grenville Estate Office in Queen Street, they operated on the principle of building leases with a ground rent paid to the Thynnes—a device often used in inherited estates so that sale of the freehold could be avoided. Following the death of Colonel Algernon Thynne in 1918, most of the farmlands in the old Stratton Manor, as well as the various leasehold interests, were sold off. Today all that remains are the memorials in Kilkhampton Church and the advowson of the living which is in the hands of the Hon John Thynne.

The Arundel lands, including Efford Manor and Strand Farm, were inherited by Sir Thomas Acland, 10th Baronet, in 1802, and it was not until this family came into the picture that any major developments took place in Bude. The Aclands, though equally ancient, have very different origins to the Norman Grenvilles and Arundels. First recorded in 1155 they were of English (Saxon) stock. At that date the family was settled at Acland (Acca's Lane) in the parish of Landkey, near Barnstaple, where they were the original freeholders who had created their own farm out of wasteland and who held it in 'socage' for the Lord of the Manor, the Bishop of Exeter. For the next seven centuries the family prospered and their lands grew, because of fortunate or discreet marriages. Like the Grenvilles and Arundels they were loyal to the Crown during the Civil War.

Liberal in outlook, the Aclands did much for Bude. They rebuilt the old Efford fish cellars into Efford Cottage where various members of the family frequently stayed, Sir Thomas himself often bringing his yacht, *The Lady of St Kilda,* into harbour. Their mark is all over Bude: Killerton Road (formerly Tagg's Lane, the sheep track to Stratton which crossed Strand Farm) and Holnicote Road are both named after Acland houses, the former near Exeter and the latter in west Somerset, both given to the National Trust, with the adjoining estates, during the present century. And there is now an Acland Close in a new housing estate off the Poughill Road.

Sir Thomas was also interested in the possibilities of Bude as a seaside resort and incidentally gave the town its first bathing pool: Sir Thomas's Bath or Pit, 'with graduated depth for gentlemen,' which is still in use at the end of the breakwater. His second son, Arthur, made up Bude's first tide-tables and was responsible for placing the half-tide cross at the end of Coach Rock on Summerleaze beach. When Sir Thomas Acland's daughter, Agnes, married Arthur Mills (MP for Taunton and later Exeter between 1857 and 1880) in 1848, they were given land on Efford Down on which was built the large red-brick Victorian mansion, now Efford Down Hotel. His successors carried on the same traditions after Sir Thomas's death in 1871. The 11th Baronet, also Sir Thomas (1809-1898) was a lifelong friend and parliamentary associate of W. E. Gladstone but retained the interest in Bude, enlarging the parish church (St Michael's) which his father had given to the town, giving land for two Non-conformist churches and founding Bude's primary school. The Acland housing developments in Bude—the Crescent, Canal Cottages (now Breakwater Road), Killerton and Holnicote Roads among them—were carried out on the building lease principle. Sir Charles Thomas Acland, the 12th Baronet, followed the same tradition in the early decades of the present century granting land for the Congregational and Roman Catholic churches.

On the death in 1939 of Sir Francis, the 14th Baronet who had at one time been MP for North Cornwall, the Acland estates in the area had to be sold to pay for death duties, but the present Baronet, Sir Richard, continued to take an interest in Bude. In 1940 he granted to the Urban District Council a 500 year lease at nominal rent, for the fine sweep of cliff-land at Compass Point, Efford Ditch and Upton. The Council had already purchased Summerleaze Down from the Thynnes who had also sold a further area of downland for use as a golf course.

The diligence of the two Bude landlords during the 19th century is quaintly, and perhaps not entirely disinterestedly, shown by Canon W. Maskell, who then lived at the castle, in *Bude Haven, A Pen and Ink Sketch,* published in 1863.

'The village of Bude lies upon two sides of a small stream which runs into the sea. It belongs chiefly to two proprietors only (Thynne and Acland), and consists upon the north side of a scattered collection of houses, some in rows, some singly extending up a moderately sloping hill (Belle Vue); upon the other of rows of houses and a pretentious looking hotel (The Falcon), a new church, the parsonage and some good cottages (Breakwater Road and The Crescent) let to visitors in the summer. The two sides are very different in character and appearance. On the one side there is small sign of care or expense in keeping the houses in repair or of attention to the wants of those who live in them, and not a few of the buildings exhibit a very narrow escape indeed from the general look of a dilapidated little Irish town. But on the other side (owned by Acland, Maskell's own landlord) every house or little row of houses, though not always built with the best taste, shows as plainly as words could tell that the careful hand and eye of a liberal landlord have been there for years.'

The 'liberal landlord' of this rather fawning paragraph was Sir Thomas Acland who had inherited the Arundel estates in Cornwall as a boy of 16. He most certainly was a great benefactor to Bude and had given strong support to the canal scheme, even having his own warehouse in the upper basin. It is, however, hardly fair to the Thynnes, though the development of their lands in Bude and their not inconsiderable benefactions came later: the site for the parish hall, for example, in 1894 and for the church of St Leonard which was never built. But the Thynnes held strongly to their Anglican beliefs and never allowed a Nonconformist church or chapel to be built on their land. The Aclands were deeply committed Anglicans too but showed a greater understanding of religious movements and the needs of others so that today the churches of four different denominations stand on what had been their land.

Two views of Stowe Barton showing the farm house which was once the stable block of the great house. ABOVE: In 1860. (JH) BELOW: Today. (RB)

ABOVE: The half-tide cross, placed on Coach Rock at Summerleaze beach by Arthur Acland in the 1840s. (RB) CENTRE: Efford Cottage in the 19th century, the Acland's home in Bude. BELOW: The same cottage today. (MM)

Field map of Stowe Barton in 1694 when it was the home farm for John Grenville. (JH, IP) INSET: The Grenville Arms above the door of Stowe Barton.

Three generations of the Acland family. LEFT: A photograph of Sir Thomas Acland, 10th Baronet, in his 80th year, 1867.
RIGHT: Sir Thomas Acland, 11th Baronet, with his wife and daughter, in the 1870s.

ABOVE: Efford Head and the downs, part of the land given to the town by Sir Richard Acland. (MM) BELOW: Trerice, the Tudor mansion built by Sir John Arundel in the 16th century, near Newquay. (A sketch by Sir Thomas Acland.)

A Considerable Trade

The traditional industries of Cornwall have always been mining, fishing and agriculture, together with various supporting trades needed to keep them going and the usual complement of domestic enterprises. The Stratton Hundred has never been an important mining area, though it has often been prospected. There is no tin. During the early 19th century, trial pits were dug for antimony on the common between Millook and Trebarfoote Manor, in the parish of Poundstock, and the metal may have been mined in a small way. It was also worked near Cancleave Strand, just south of Millook, and there were shareholders' meetings at the Hundred of Stratton Inn at Wainhouse Corner. There is said to have been a copper mine in the parish of Morwenstowe about 1580 but no details are known. Some copper was certainly extracted from Wheal Morwenna in the same parish, probably near Stanbury Farm, in 1845; and A. K. Hamilton Jenkyn in *Mines and Miners of Cornwall*, 1970, tells that in 1827 'a fine copper mine had recently been set to work in the neighbourhood of Bude' with a lode under the sea, and that four tons of copper 'had already been raised by one man and a boy'. No signs of this enterprise remain today. The absence of mining on a large scale meant that the area escaped the depression of the 1860s when thousands of unemployed Cornish miners emigrated.

The coast has always been too rough and rugged and the harbours either too difficult or simply non-existent for fishing in small boats to have been practicable except sporadically, but when the shoals of pilchard or mackerel appeared, farmers and labourers left their fields and took to the sea. Even so, in the 18th century and possibly earlier there must have been sufficient fishing off Bude Haven to justify the existence of the Efford fish cellars, and possibly others elsewhere on the coast. In such cellars, fish were either smoked or pickled in salt from local pans.

From an early date, agriculture was largely based on grain cultivation (wheat, barley, oats) with small tough sheep on the moors, commons and open cliff-lands. Rabbits were warrened; a notable site on Grenville land a short way south of Duckpool still bears the name Warren Gutter. Enclosures seem to have followed an erratic pattern as the shape and size of fields has been dictated largely by topography and the need for shelter. Few parts of the Hundred were suitable for the large open-field cultivation so common elsewhere in Britain but there is some evidence of past 'stitch' tenure. The acreage under cultivation increased markedly in the late 18th century when the potato came into general use, much waste land being reclaimed and put permanently to agriculture. Moorland areas such as Greenamoor, near Week St Mary, and Wrasford, north of Kilkhampton, were then much reduced in size. Fertilizers (mainly sea-weed, sea-sand and a rudimentary form of fish-meal) were increasingly used. It is not known when garlic was first cultivated but it long supported a small export trade.

Outside events have always influenced the economics of farming. A slump followed the end of the Napoleonic Wars (1815) and in Stratton, where there were no fishing or mining industries to compete with agriculture, farm wages remained as low as 7s per week until the middle of the century. The result was some emigration to mining areas and to Canada. Agricultural Unions in Stratton opposed the new Poor Laws; an attitude which led to rioting so that in 1837 troops had to be called out to protect the commissioners. There was further rioting and emigration during the 'Hungry Forties', a decaying period for British agriculture, before the Corn Laws were repealed in 1846.

As well as the tidal mills at Efford and Hele, there were water-mills at Howard in Stratton, higher up the River Neet at Bush, at Millook and in the Coombe Valley where the great wheel may still be seen. There were windmills at Prestacott in Launcells and at Marhamchurch. There were also fulling-mills, or tucking-mills as they were known in Cornwall, at Jacobstowe, Week St Mary and Poundstock, whose name derives from *Pound* meaning mill and *stoc*, a place. These were part of a wool industry based upon local sheep, whose wool was improving over the centuries with improved husbandry and better land management. Hand-spun and hand-woven cloth, known as *kersey,* was made at Stratton and elsewhere. There were also three yards for tanning hides in the Hundred: in Week St Mary and Stratton. Among other small industries were lime-kilns, quarries for sand-stone and, on the culm measures, for brick-clay. There was also a foundry in Marhamchurch, founded in the 1740s by the Box family and producing work which can still be seen in the area. Parts of the main building still stand, now converted into dwellings. There were blacksmiths' shops in most villages and the usual range of common rural crafts.

Bude Haven had been a port long before the canal was ever thought of. The Grenvilles had appointed a Master of the Port of Bude, one Simon Symmons, as early as 1535; and to this day Grenville Quay Cottage above Nanny Moore's Bridge indicates an old quay. William Borlase (1754) described it as being merely a sandy creek for small vessels. But an entry in *The Universal British Directory* of 1791 reads:

'Two miles from Stratton is Bude Harbour belonging to the port of Padstow where there has of late years been a considerable trade carried on in exporting corn, particularly oats, to different parts of the Kingdom and vast quantities of bark to Ireland; and importing coals and salt, the former from Wales and the latter from Bristol. There are large and commodious cellars built to receive goods imported which are forwarded almost immediately to the owners.'

The bark exported to Ireland was used for tanning. Ships, mostly flat-bottomed, were beached on the sand when the tide ebbed. Their cargoes were unloaded direct into horse-drawn carts which were then taken either to the various cellars around the haven or further inland to Stratton and beyond. A trade grew up in groceries from Bristol, known locally as 'Bristol goods'. As well as coal, limestone was brought to the haven from South Wales, burnt in the Efford lime-kilns and used mainly for mortar.

Although Borlase had ideas about canals in north Cornwall as early as 1750, the Bude canal itself was not considered until 1774 when the idea was to connect the haven with the navigable reaches of the Tamar and so with the English Channel. An Act of Parliament was passed, capital was authorized and a meandering line surveyed by Edmund Leach. The project was abandoned when John Smeaton, who had studied the canal system of Holland, pointed out that while physically possible it was economically unattractive. A few years later Leach suggested the use of inclined planes with 'mechanical hydraulic machines' to move barges from one level to another. Nothing was done, however, until the 3rd Earl Stanhope, who owned land at Holsworthy, re-opened the subject. Another route was surveyed; the earlier suggestion of steam engines with vertical lifts and a multiplicity of locks was scrapped in favour of 'iron rail-roads' designed to work alongside the canal. Stanhope preferred small boats, suspended between two wheels and drawn by horses, as the best means of overcoming hilly sections of the route. But nothing happened. In 1795, Roger Fulton, an American engineer, advised wooden boats with wheels and a double inclined plane working by counterbalance; the weight of the descending boat, augmented by water power, would pull the ascending boat up the plane. Among the possible ways of applying water-power, one of Fulton's suggestions was the 'well and bucket' method later used at Hobbacott Down.

The Napoleonic Wars and international tension caused the project to be postponed yet again. But the idea was revived in 1814, thanks to local initiative and the continued support of Stanhope who unfortunately died before anything more happened. However, the 4th Earl remained interested; James Green (engineer) and Thomas Shearm (surveyor) were commissioned to work out a new line, and in April 1918 their report was accepted. They recommended a canal 19 feet wide with boats of five tons and inclined planes to move them up and down the hills. The construction of a breakwater was recommended, to stand 10 feet above the level of the spring tides and connect Chapel Rock with the mainland. They also advised that the channel of the River Neet be altered and a sea lock built.

The line recommended and eventually followed went up the valley to Hele Bridge, and was wide enough to take barges carrying 40 tons of sand, used as a manure in the surrounding countryside, though in the event the barges had a capacity of only 20 tons. From Hele Bridge the canal went on to near modern Red Post where it branched, one arm leading to Holsworthy with an aqueduct across the Tamar, another following the Tamar valley to Druxton, near Launceston, and a feeder line to carry the canal's water supply from a reservoir (now known as Tamar Lake) at Alfardisworthy above Kilkhampton. Wharves were built at the terminals and other centres but the canal was never extended eastwards from Holsworthy as Green had urged. Its purpose was to facilitate trade in sand, to carry coal and to assist the export of timber, charcoal and agricultural produce.

The first inclined plane which led from Hele Bridge to Marhamchurch (120 ft vertical and 830 ft long) was powered by a water-wheel. The next at Hobbacott Down (225 ft and 935 ft) used Fulton's 'well and bucket' method. Two wells were sunk from the top of this plane to the level of the bottom. Huge buckets

(10 ft diameter, 3½ ft deep and carrying 15 tons of water) were suspended in each well and linked together by chains over a drum-wheel. The descending bucket supplied the necessary power to raise a tub-boat loaded with five tons of sand or other goods from one level to the other in remarkably short time. As the bucket hit the bottom, a valve opened automatically to allow the water to escape. Chains were liable to break and accidents were fairly frequent but the system worked. Four other shorter planes were powered by water-wheels: Venla (58 ft vertical 500 ft long) Merrifield (60 ft, 360 ft) Tamerton (55 ft, 360 ft) and Werrington (51 ft, 259 ft).

An Act of Parliament was secured in 1819, and the Bude Harbour and Canal Company was formed with Earl and Countess Stanhope, Sir Arscott Molesworth, Sir Thomas Acland, George Gale (the original chairman) and James Green among the shareholders. The original estimate for the whole canal and all harbour improvements was £128,341; the eventual cost came to roughly £120,000 (authorised capital £95,000). Work started in July 1819, when Stanhope laid the first stone of the breakwater.

In spite of technical and financial difficulties, the harbour and canal were officially opened for trade in July 1823. Within a short distance of the sea-lock there were three wharves: the sand-wharf with a rail running down to the beach, the Company's wharf alongside the main basin and Sir Thomas Acland's private wharf. Sir Thomas took a leading part in the enterprise, the seaward parts of which were on his land, by seeing to the planting of trees on Efford Down to protect the basins from the prevailing wind, providing some of the materials and building (about 1825) a large coaching inn, the Falcon, with a terrace of cottages for canal workers; Breakwater Road cottages followed. A wooden swing-bridge over the canal led to a new road (the Crescent) across the marshes and terminated in a bridge, later known as Bencoolen Bridge, with a toll-house which still stands. A subsidiary canal from Hele Bridge to a point somewhere in the middle of what is now Killerton Road was suggested but never built.

The harbour still looks much as it did in 1823. The old lime kilns and fish cellars were already in the process of being replaced by the cottages which now look into the lock, though the original sea-lock and canal basin had to be enlarged in 1835. The first breakwater, with its steep sides and imposing pier head was almost destroyed in a storm in February 1838. Rebuilt the following year by the Company's engineer (George Casebourne) to a design by

ABOVE: The earliest known picture of Bude, an 18th century water colour. In the centre is Efford Mill built by the Arundells in 1589. On the right is Bude Bridge, renamed Nanny Moore's Bridge in the 19th century. LEFT: The water mill in the Coombe Valley. (RB) RIGHT: Another old water mill, this time at Millook, c1910. (AJ) BELOW: A Bude smack above the swing-bridge, before the lifeboat house was built in 1863.

Mill, Millook

James Walker, the new (and present) breakwater was much less pretentious than its predecessor. Standing only four feet above the high water mark of a spring tide, the angle is lower and resistance to the waves minimal. Some stone was brought by sea from the Vale of Lanherne, once the home of a branch of the Arundel family. Sir Thomas Acland again gave much of the material, and it was about then that he provided the small bathing pool, which bears his name, and the Storm Tower above Compass Point.

For 30 years or more all went well with the canal. Inland farms and the growing harbour town prospered. All heavy goods needed in the area came by sea and were distributed inland by way of the canal. But the Railway Age and the development of chemical fertilizers soon killed the venture, the railway reaching Launceston in 1864, Holsworthy in 1879 and Bude in 1898. Canal barges and tub-boats which carried 59,620 tons in 1838 moved only 22,807 in 1888. The sand-railway continued to function until 1942 when lorries took over from cart-horses.

It was the same with shipping. During the heyday of the canal trade 40 or 50 vessels made Bude their home port, some with names which exuded confidence: *Endeavour* with Captain Sluggett, *Tavy* with Captain Mountjoy, *Venerable* with Captain Owen. 151 vessels of up to 50 tons burden traded in and out of Bude in 1825, 315 in 1846, 241 in 1865, 187 in 1885 and 145 in 1900. Numbers continued to decline until the last of the trading ketches, *Ceres*, finally sank in 1936. For nearly 30 years thereafter the harbour was rarely used and the UDC began to think seriously about closing it down. But then local interest in fishing began to grow and visiting yachtsmen called more frequently.

In 1891, Bude-Stratton UDC took over Tamar Lake as a water supply — it has now been replaced by a reservoir a short distance up the infant River Tamar, and is used for fishing in the summer and bird-watching in the winter. Ten years later another Act of Parliament (The Stratton and Bude Improvement Act) authorized sale to the Council of the remaining Canal Company assets. The figure was £8,000. The Company had paid few dividends during its life of nearly 80 years but it did pay its debts. Charles Hadfield, the leading authority on British canals, has summed it up:

'It was a remarkable piece of engineering, the longest tub-boat canal in Britain and that with the most inclined planes. It was a conception which outran the day to day reliability and strength of the materials available.'

ABOVE: Beyond the lock gates, Efford Cottage and the breakwater. CENTRE: Past the breakwater, going towards Chapel Rock. (RIC) BELOW: A 19th century print of St Michael's Church and Canal Cottages.

ABOVE: A view of Bude harbour from below Chapel Rock and a warning to swimmers. (RIC) LEFT: A sand barge used on the canal during the 19th century. (RB) RIGHT: Sand rail on Summerleaze beach, discovered in 1979 after the gales and flooding of the River Neet. (RB)

ABOVE: The swing bridge across the canal. (MM)
CENTRE: Bude canal; the building on the left was used first
as a saw-mill, then a laundry and later as a council store.
(MM) BELOW: A schooner and ketches in the canal, c1912.
(BSHFE)

ABOVE: The original Bude breakwater with its pier head—destroyed by a storm in 1839. CENTRE: Looking across the canal from Falcon Hotel to the castle, recently completed. BELOW: The canal and Summerleaze beach before building of Breakwater Road Cottages. A sand-barge is on the canal and the sand railway beyond. (Sketches by Sir Thomas Acland.)

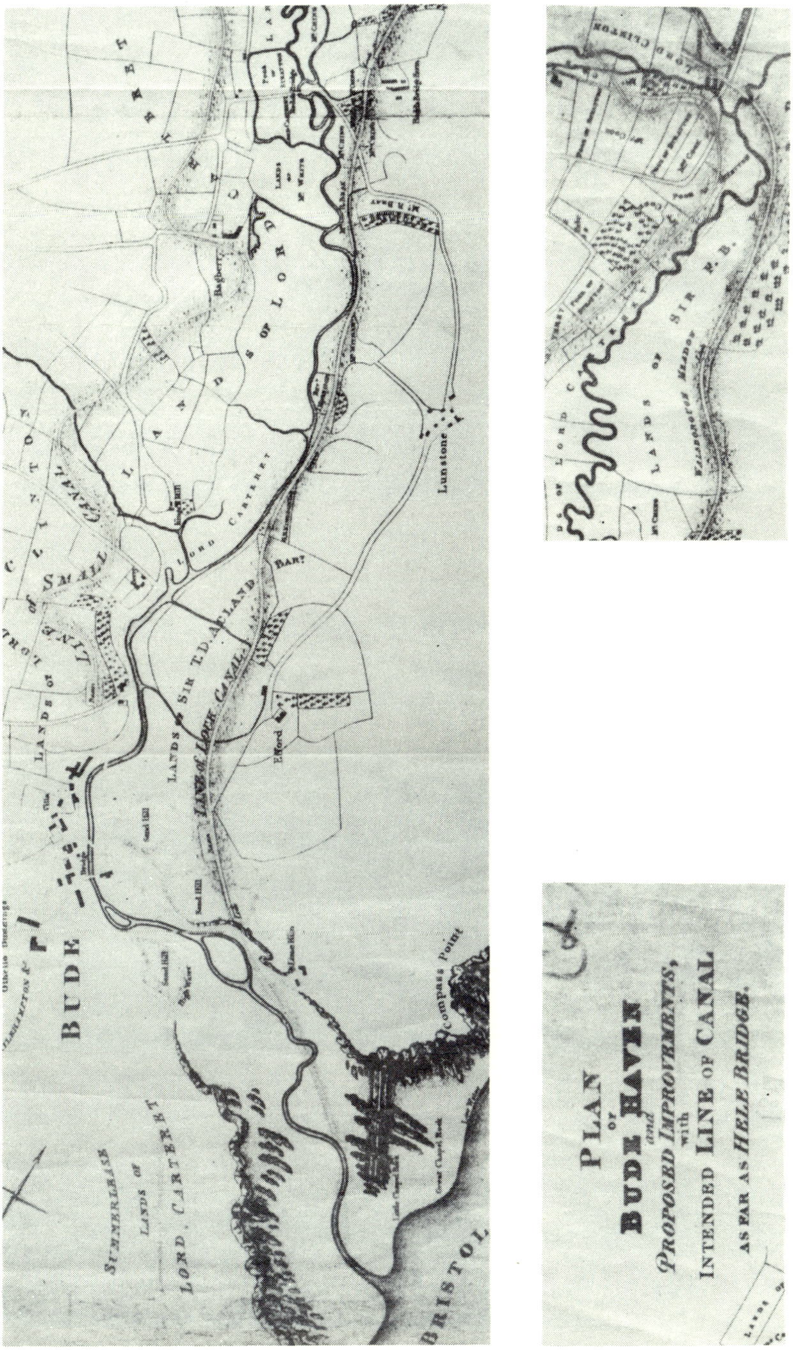

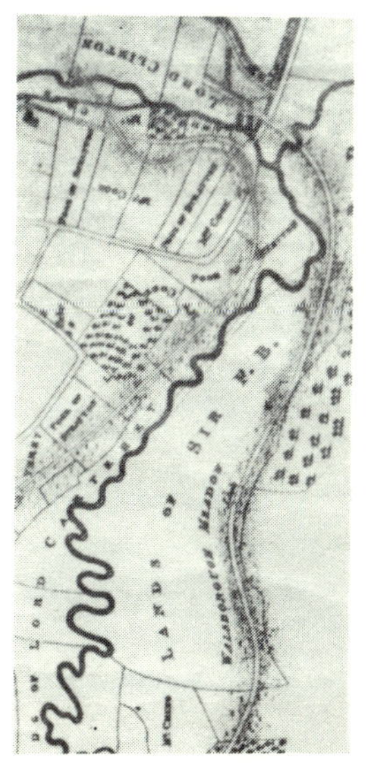

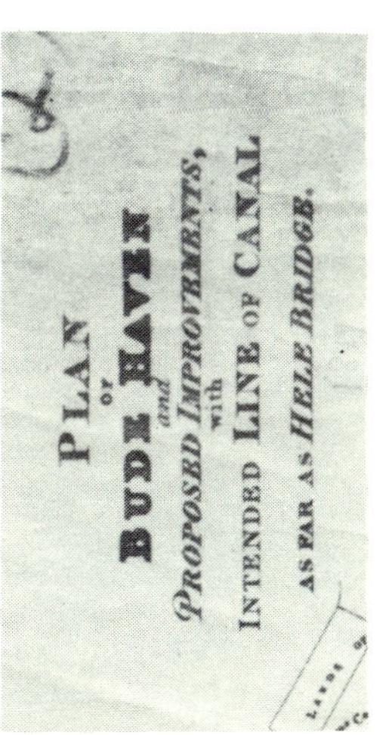

A map shewing the proposed improvement of the canal after the survey of 1817.

ABOVE: Ships waiting to enter Bude canal under the lee of
the breakwater, c1890 and BELOW: waiting to leave the
canal. (MM)

64

The Cruel Coast

The north Cornwall coast is one of the most treacherous in England largely because, in nautical terms, it is a lee shore: if engines fail or sails break down, ships are literally blown on to the rocks by the prevailing south-westerly winds. There is no easy refuge between Hartland Point and Padstow, a distance of about 40 miles, though Bude Haven did afford some refuge. Even after the breakwater was built it remained a hazardous harbour to enter by reason not only of rough seas but also awkward tides. Ships seldom came in without help from the 'hobblers' who met them outside the harbour in an open rowing boat. The 'hobblers' not only acted as pilot but took ropes from the vessel and made these fast to the warping posts along the channel.

Long before this, in 1602, Richard Carew described the haven as 'an open sandy bay, in whose mouth riseth a little hill, by every sea-flood made an island and thereon a decayed chapel. It spareth road only to such small shipping as bring the tide with them and leaveth them dry when the ebb hath carried away the salt water.' The chapel, which was dedicated to St Michael, stood on Chapel Rock, now linked to the shore by the breakwater, and was occupied by the hermit who kept a fire burning to guide mariners.

Records of wrecks along the Bude coast go back over many centuries. In November 1467, the *Raphael* of Bristol, homeward bound from Danzig, was driven ashore near Duckpool, below the great house of Stowe. Cargo and gear, valued at £1,000, had come into the hands of three local men who refused to return it. More cargo was carried away by others, though it was uncertain whether or not the ship was technically a wreck. A complicated legal wrangle followed as the owner, John May of Bristol sought to reclaim his goods. The outcome is not recorded, but the tale has become a familiar one. John Bray, of Poughill, who centuries later wrote *An Account of Wrecks, 1759-1830* gives the details of numerous cargoes 'picked up' from the foreshore. When a small sloop loaded with casks of gin was wrecked about 1770, the captain gave to one John Heard for his Christmas feast at Slade in

Poughill 'a barrel of gin and one had plenty to drink that night, and the captain was very merry.' At least this wreck does not seem to have been the usual tragedy.

The *Bencoolen* in October 1862 was perhaps the most famous of all Bude wrecks and has given rise to Bencoolen Bridge over the River Neet and to more than one house-name; one of the houses so named was built by Oliver Davy, a local shipowner. The *Bencoolen*, a steamer of 1415 tons, had no connection with Bude but was on her way from Liverpool to Bombay with a cargo of iron telegraph poles. In heavy seas she drifted helplessly, and broadside on, onto Summerleaze beach to become a total wreck. The captain had retired drunk to his cabin and was drowned with 29 others from a crew of 32. The lifeboat could not be launched but a rocket-line was fired across the ship and a raft eventually launched. The figurehead is displayed in the town museum and the ship's bell, in the Methodist Chapel at Roscarrock.

Not long after this wreck a Spanish vessel, *Juanita*, laden with sugar, was driven on to the rocks at Duckpool. With the help of a rope, the coastguard officer forced his way through the waves and climbed on board where he found, to his surprise, the captain standing at bay in his cabin, drawn sword in hand. He had no intention of handing over his ship to Cornish wreckers of whom he had heard so many stories. But the coastguard managed to reassure him and the rest of his crew, and all were saved. The coastguard was subsequently presented with a Sword of Honour by the Queen of Spain, and the coxswain of the Bude lifeboat received a gold medal from the Spanish government.

Between 1862 and 1900 there were more than 80 strandings in Bude Bay, and at least 70 lives were lost. During December 1894, three ships—*Elter Water* of Dublin, *Tullochorum* of Plymouth and the schooner, *Robert*, from Norway—were wrecked in a single week. Another famous wreck was *Capricorno*, an Austrian barque taking coal from Cardiff to the Adriatic. She was driven onto the rocks near the breakwater on 20 December 1900, and out of a crew of 14 only two survived. At an enquiry held by the Board of Trade, the people of Bude were completely exonerated from any 'suggestion that they had been guilty of want of humanity—a suggestion which to anyone who knows the people of the place, could have seemed ludicrous had it not been so wantonly cruel,' (C. F. Croxton in *Bencoolen to Capricorno—a History of Bude Wrecks*).

These sea dramas, which happened so frequently, affected both old and young in the community. James Arthur, then headmaster of the elementary school, wrote in his diary for 25 October 1865: 'The total wreck of the *Georgina*, of Glasgow, has completely upset the school today. Following this the children were out before time yesterday; the school is almost reduced to nothing through the wreck.'

Thanks to the coming of steamships and oil engines and the falling off of trade with the port of Bude, wrecks have occurred less frequently during the present century but they have still occurred. In February 1904, *Wild Pigeon* was carried away from her mooring in the canal when the inner lock-gate was broken by a huge wave. Also early in this century, the schooner *Crystal Spring* was wrecked off the end of the breakwater with a cargo of coal which was much appreciated by the people of Bude. The *Llandaff*, a steamship from Cardiff, somehow ended up with her bow high in the air over the end of Sir Thomas's Pit. More fortunate than most, she eventually refloated herself after the crew had been saved. Even today dramas occasionally occur: a Swansea tug, *Fusee II*, broke down in Barnstaple Bay in 1970, drifted towards Bude and beached herself on Summerleaze sands. There she was salvaged and refloated by Captain Herbert and a local crew and brought into harbour.

The tradition of wreckers and smugglers dies hard, though it is difficult to separate fact from fable, most stories probably being a combination of the two. The late 18th century wrecker, 'Cruel Copinger', almost certainly did operate in his schooner, *Black Prince,* from a base in Marsland Mouth near Morwenstowe. Then there is the troubled spirit of the Widemouth Bay wrecker, Featherstone, which is traditionally described as being imprisoned beneath Black Rock at the south end of the bay, only to be released should he succeed in weaving a rope of sand.

It is doubtful if much smuggling was carried out on this wild and open coast so different from the sheltered woody creeks of south Cornwall, lying within easy reach of France, but it certainly did occur. A smuggling frigate, *Two Cherubs,* is said to have been based at Bude with a one legged villain, Simon Symonds, as the man in charge. The King's man, John Silver, caught Symonds red-handed one day and had his head cut off with a cutlass for his pains. The body was lashed to Silver's own white horse and driven into the sea, and the head was buried in the wall of Grenville Cottage; at every crescent moon three taps at the door are heard when the headless body returns to seek its head. Fanciful maybe, but a skull is reputed to have been found built into the cottage wall. The figurehead of the *Two Cherubs,* said to have been carved by Grinling Gibbons in 1663, is now in the museum of the Cutty Sark Preservation Society.

Bude Bay used to be covered by His Majesty's Customs House at Padstow. Clashes between smugglers and excise men did undoubtedly take place, and one happened at Millook on 11 November 1820. Excise men under Sampson Woodcock seized 400 'tubs of foreign run spirits.' Crews from the smuggling cutter, which then appeared, started firing on the beach. Preventive men returned fire until their ammunition was finished, whereupon the smugglers came ashore, attacked Woodcock and his men, forced them to retreat and carried off the six-oared galley belonging to the station. Encounters did not always end in violence. In January 1831, preventive men at Bude observed a suspicious looking sail in the offing and set off in pursuit after impressing a couple of volunteers. They approached the strange vessel, whose crew acted in such an odd way that the preventive men began to have visions of tubs of brandy and rolls of tobacco. Lured on by such hopes, they boarded their prize without meeting resistance. Convinced that they had a valuable trophy, they brought her triumphantly into harbour only to find a cargo of salt herrings and nothing else. The master, who had not informed them of their error, expressed gratitude for 'this kindly re-enforcement of his own weary crew in bringing his vessel to port.'

According to RNLI records a lifeboat, believed to have been sent from Plymouth Dockyard, was stationed at Bude for a short time in 1817 but allowed to fall into disrepair. A Mortar Life Saving Apparatus came to Bude in 1827, forerunner of the Rocket Apparatus in 1852. The next lifeboat, usually considered to be the first and known as the *Royal William*, was a bladder boat given by King William IV in 1837. She was unstable and capsized while on exercises in the harbour when two of her crew were drowned. In 1853 she was replaced by one of the new self-righting boats, and ten years later the lifeboat house near the Falcon Hotel was built with funds provided by the family of Elizabeth Moore Garden and on land given by Sir Thomas Acland. The next lifeboat was a gift from the Garden family and was appropriately named *Elizabeth Moore Garden* as were the next two boats in 1886 and 1911. The latter was withdrawn in 1923, not replaced but served for a spell in Scotland after leaving Bude.

Launching the lifeboat was always a problem. Taking the boat down the canal and through the lock-gates was a lengthy process, only possible if the tide and weather conditions allowed. The alternative method was to take the boat to the sea on a special launching carriage drawn by ten cart-horses—a difficult task but a superb sight as the great horses galloped into the waves. After 1852, the lifeboat was backed by the Rocket Apparatus, kept in the Rocket House at the end of Breakwater Road, and manned by coastguards. This invention by a Cornishman, Mr Trengrouse of Helston, enabled a line to be fired onto a stranded ship, so establishing a link with the shore. Rescue could then be carried out by means of a breeches-buoy.

The story of the Bude lifeboat is one of courage and success: 70 lives were saved, as well as another 90 by rocket, but not without cost to the crews. One of the early coxswains, Maynard, was drowned while his crew rescued sailors from the ketch *Elizabeth Scown* which ran aground in a severe gale while coming into harbour with a load of stone for the extension to St Michael's Church. Maynard's act was described at the time as being of almost insane heroism. For some 40 years after 1923 there was no lifeboat at Bude but then an Inshore Rescue Boat Station was established near the lock gates. A fine tradition has been inherited by those who man the RNLI Inshore Rescue Boat.

But what of the ships themselves and the men who owned and sailed them? In the years around 1800, Captain Moyse of Stratton traded in 'Bristol goods' between Bude and Bristol using his sloop *Mayflower,* no sign of which remains. Nor is there any trace of the old ale-house, The Jolly Sailor, run by Nanny Wilson on the site of the present Globe Hotel. Later in the 19th century there was the ketch *Alford,* owned by John Banbury of Bude with J. B. Cook as master; and *Clara May* owned for many years by John Cornish and later by a partnership which included the Parkhouse family. Many of the old sea-captains lived in Breakwater Road, once known as Canal Terrace, where several of the cottages are named after ships ie: Jessamine and Hazel.

Boats were occasionally built in Bude before the opening of the canal but exactly where this was done is not known. Two shipyards were later opened beside the canal, the most successful and long lasting being the yard established by Robert Stapleton in 1830 and worked by his family and descendants for the best part of a century. A major problem was how to heave the old wooden ships out of the canal for repair or re-furbishing, an operation, according to Stapleton, needing plenty of 'main strength and foolishness'. As the basin was restricted in size, ships had to be launched sideways into the canal and removed from the water in the same way.

To heave a ship out of the water, she was first rolled over on to her side and held in position by heavily loaded canal barges. She was then taken to the verge of the canal opposite the yard and winched ashore, broadside on, up a specially prepared and greased slipway until she was standing upright and clear of the water. Work could then be carried out: caulking, replacing damaged planks or stern-posts or whatever work was needed. At least a dozen ships were built in Stapleton's yard alongside the upper basin: among them were *Mirre, Annie Davey, Elizabeth Scown, Affo, Sir Thomas Acland* and *Lady Acland*. The largest was *Annie Davey* (73 tons) built in 1872. *Ceres* was taken out of the water several times as was the ketch *Lady Acland*. Built in 1835, she underwent major repairs in the yard in 1904 when she was renamed *Agnes,* after Lady Acland's daughter. She continued to trade in and out of Bude through World War II and survived until 1955 when she was finally wrecked in the West Indies. Near the shipyard, the Bude Haven Steam Saw Mill was set up to provide timber for the ships. As canal trade fell, the building was sold (c1900) to Arthur Venning who started the Bude Steam Laundry. The building is now a council store.

The best known of all Bude ketches was *Ceres*, built at Salcombe in 1811 and lengthened in Stapleton's yard in 1868. She was owned by the Petherick family of Bude for four generations, and when she finally sank in the Bristol Channel in 1936, she had been for many years the oldest vessel on Lloyd's register. She carried military stores for Wellington's armies on the coast of Spain during the Peninsular War and 101 years after being commissioned had her first engine fitted, though used only in emergencies. After coming to Bude in 1826 she sailed regularly to Liverpool and various continental and North Sea ports. She was caught in the great gale of 1891 while sailing from Padstow to Plymouth with a cargo of slates and managed to round Land's End safely as few ships under sail were able to do in the conditions. She was nearly wrecked in 1900 but was saved by a tug which took her into Padstow harbour. *Ceres* sailed these seas for 125 years, 100 under unassisted sail, without drowning a single member of her successive crews; and it is calculated that she must have carried a quarter of a million tons of cargo.

ABOVE: On board the *Clara May,* a Bude ketch. (BSHFE)
BELOW: The *Elizabeth* among the rocks of Sharpnose Point,
16 February 1912. (RST)

71

The *Ceres* with the hobblers in attendance, 1912 (A) and
INSET: rounding Barrel Rock at the end of the breakwater
in a heavy sea. (RST)

ABOVE: The lower wharf crowded with shipping, c1904.
(MM) CENTRE: The wreckage of the *Bencoolen* in 1862.
BELOW: The wreck of the *Georgina* off Sharpnose Point in
1865. (MS)

ABOVE: SS *Llandaff* lying over the end of Sir Thomas's Pit 1899. CENTRE: The *Wild Pigeon* stranded after the inner lock-gate had been destroyed by huge waves in February 1904. (RST) BELOW: Another stranded vessel, this time the *Alford* in 1908. (RST)

ABOVE: The *Ant* awash. BELOW: The *Crystal Spring* on the rocks. (BSHFE)

ABOVE LEFT: The figurehead of the *William Tapscott,*
wrecked at Bude in 1888, (BSHFE) and RIGHT: figurehead
from the *Bencoolen.* (BSHFE) BELOW: The lifeboat and
lifeboathouse c1890. (MM)

Views of the lifeboat. ABOVE: With crew c1890; (MS)
CENTRE: being paraded along the Strand 1904. (RST)
BELOW: The *Elizabeth Moore Garden 2* in Bude Bay 1905.
(RST)

ABOVE: The third *Elizabeth Moore Garden* soon after it was brought to Bude in 1911. (RST) CENTRE: Launching a lifeboat with the aid of horses c1904. (MM) BELOW: Another launching, this time into the canal c1920. (BSHFE)

ABOVE: Stratton in 1880; the churchyard was extended considerably after this house was demolished. The couple on the left, Mr and Mrs Dell, lived in the left-hand cottage. (AJ) CENTRE: A Stratton gathering c1890. BELOW: The Bay Tree Inn, Old Stratton. (AJ)

Gem of the West

The *Universal British Directory* (1791) gives a vivid picture of Stratton as the 19th century was approaching: 'The cross post arrives on Mondays, Thurdays and Saturdays from Holsworthy. Blatchfords waggon departs from Exeter for the Tree Inn every Tuesday.' The gentry for that year were listed as John King, Mr Martin, Mr Oliver and Miss Martha Uglow. Rev John King was vicar with Thomas Lukey, druggist and Mr Juke and Mr King, physicians. Traders listed included Edmund Badcock, excise officer; John Bailey, hatter; Mrs Ballhatchet, dealer in clothes; James Bickle, tailor; Samuel Bray, schoolmaster; Thomas Ching, tanner; Thomas Dawe, cordwainer; George Elias, peruke (wig) maker; John Martyn, victualler; George Uglow, clockmaker; William Wonnacott, saddler; and Capt Robert Moise, trader from Bristol to Bude in his sloop *Enterprise:* a remarkably self-sufficient community, little touched by the passage of time.

While the church dominated Stratton in the late 18th century, there were also more than twelve ale-houses and inns including the Ackland Arms, Bay Tree Inn, Bideford Inn, Butchers Arms, Commercial Inn, Cornish Inn or One and All and Fifteen Bells, Glovers Arms, Griffin, Kings Arms, Market Inn, New Inn, Poughill Inn, Ring O'Bells, Ship Inn, Three Tens and the Tree Inn; all for a population of about 900. In Jubilee Square there was a building known as Church House, not normally inhabited but occupied when the wardens brewed beer which was sold and drunk on the spot, the revenue going to the church. When the fair was being held, Church House was let to merchants, gypsies and their dancing bear. Law and order were taken care of by the preventive officer, who was supervised by the Justices of the Peace. A jail existed near the churchyard but was moved to the old market place, off Maiden Street. The door of the 'Clink' is preserved in the church porch.

A police station was built in 1863, to be followed by a cottage hospital in 1866 and almshouses in 1910. A Union Poor House had been established in 1856 not without opposition. An earlier move in this direction resulted in serious rioting, when a mob led by Thomas Jago protested against the building, on the grounds that it would be a burden on the rates.

Throughout the 19th century Bude was growing but remained dependent upon Stratton for most things. 'A sailor', wrote Canon Maskell in 1872, 'enquired as to a doctor in Bude. ''Well, sir,'' he was told, ''you see when the quality's here in the summer us sends across to Stratton but in winter us just dies a natural death.'' ' There is often an air of superiority in 19th century writing about Bude, as for example, in *Highways and Byways in Devon and Cornwall* by Arthur Norway in 1897:
'The traveller who is wise will give a wide berth to Bude with its unsafe harbour and its new hotels and seek out Stratton that ancient town which lies fast decaying in a hollow of the hills no more than a mile and a half away ... Nowhere in Cornwall are the cottages more picturesque, the streets more narrow or more obviously ancient'.

Even today Stratton remains much as it has been through the centuries, a small market town proud of its identity and jealous of interference from outside.

Sea bathing had almost as much to do with the growth of Bude as had shipping. The Arscott family from Tetcott built The Villa in 1775 as a seaside residence for the summer; and before the turn of the century two or three families from Launceston regularly came to Bude for the purpose of bathing. They probably lodged over one of the few shops in the place, one of which sold earthenware pots and pans, another groceries. It is doubtful if they stayed at the Jolly Sailor, a little inn on the site of the Globe Hotel, which sold ale and spirits to sailors and the carters who came to the haven to collect coal and sand. Some may have stayed at the Bude Hotel which is believed to have opened in 1780.

In 1808, a clergyman named Warner wrote that many gentry and invalids from Launceston and elsewhere in eastern Cornwall came to bathe and breathe the sea air. 'There was a decent inn and several neat lodging houses for the accommodation of visitors' but with 'the resort not yet having arrived at the refinement of bathing machines, the ladies were put to some little inconvenience in performing the rites of immersion'. This was before the opening of the canal and when ships were still being unloaded on the shore when the tide was out, but the word 'resort' had already appeared.

Although bathing machines, drawn by horses to the edge of the water, did not come into use until 1846, a map of the Haven published 10 years earlier is boldly captioned 'Bude Haven which, under the patronage of Sir T. D. Acland, Bart, has lately become the fashionable Watering Place of the West.' The map shows that King Street and the east side of Lansdown Hill had already been built up but that Belle Vue was not yet complete. There was Othello Terrace with the Canal Company offices on the site now occupied by the International Stores, the terrace presumably being named after the ship *Othello* wrecked off Bude in 1808. Along the Strand were two warehouse buildings and the new Tapson's Terrace which still exists. To the south of the River Neet we see the castle, Efford Mill, the recently completed chapel of St Michael, Efford Cottage, the Falcon Hotel and Terrace and Efford Manor. The Crescent Cottages, then known as South Terrace or rudely as 'Frying Pan Row', were about to be built. Belle Vue Terrace, Hartland Terrace and some cottages on the site now occupied by Grenville Hotel followed in the 1850s-60s.

Long before the railway reached Bude, the place was reasonably well served by coaches. *Piggot and Co's Directory* for 1844 lists *Defiance*, making an 8 am start and running from Exeter to the Falcon Hotel three times each week. And the 1875 *Coombes' Guide* lists three services: the *Flying Dutchman*, leaving the Falcon at 10.00 am for Barnstaple to catch the 3.30 pm train for Paddington; the *Queen* leaving Bude Hotel for Okehampton and the train for Waterloo; and the *Standard* which took passengers to Launceston and a Plymouth connection. Four years later, the railway reached Holsworthy, a shorter coach trip to Bude.

As early as 1844, Stratton had begun to press for a railway; and as soon as the London and South Western reached Holsworthy a local committee was formed which in 1888 evolved into the Holsworthy and Bude Railway Company. By 31 January 1890 the first sod was cut by the wife of Canon Thynne, on the proposed station site at Berries Farm. The Stratton Brass Band paraded under C. H. Rattenbury, a large evergreen arch inscribed 'Welcome' and 'A Better Day' was set up and a vast lunch consumed in the Assembly Rooms—the present Villa Hall. A Commemorative Programme was produced which opened enthusiastically with the lines:

> 'Most Beautiful Bude, the Gem of the West
> Thy lovely surroundings all make the best,
> Thy views o'er the sea, the coast or inland
> Are romantic, sublime and delightfully grand.'

The original route included a station for Stratton and an extensive viaduct across the River Neet at Howard Mill. The contract date for completion was to be October 1891, but something went wrong and the scheme was abandoned. In desperation, the Stratton Trade Association approached L & SWR direct. A new and less costly route was surveyed by-passing Stratton, the Association 'magnanimously refraining from opposition', and the work went ahead. The great day came on 10 August 1898; directors arrived from Exeter in a special train and drove in open carriages through triumphal arches, which proclaimed 'Progress' and 'Success Railway', to the parish hall. The recently formed Bude band played popular music, toasts and speeches went on until late afternoon, and even the weather was kind—a great day for Bude if not for Stratton.

The arrival of the railway set the stage for the Thynne Estates to develop their part of Bude. Summerleaze Crescent, Morwenna Terrace, Burn View and Queen Street were built, largely of alien red brick brought in by the railway. To crown their idea of a Victorian watering place, the Thynnes planned a vast new hotel, The Granville, to be built on Summerleaze Down near the cricket ground. The hotel, allotted to Mr George Brendon, was to have 150 rooms, numerous suites, billiard rooms, lifts, telephones and 'accessories'. These grandiose plans ignored the controversy which had rumbled on for years over possible infringement of public rights on the downs. Foster Mellior, a member of the newly formed town council, led the opposition. The people of Bude had been told, he pointed out, that the last house on Summerleaze Crescent would be the final one to be built in the area; yet now the downs were threatened. The real issue was that the commoners saw their rights to graze donkeys being infringed by the Lord of the Manor. After prolonged and complex legal argument, the donkeys won, and the scheme was abandoned. Ironically it was Foster Mellior's wife who eventually, on 16 November 1909, laid the foundation stone of the present Grenville Hotel on its site well away from the downs. Except for the Headland Pavilion and the Picture House on the perimeter, no buildings have been erected on the downs.

A *Directory and Visitors List* was published each week during the season by Thorn's Library in the Crescent. All interests were catered for. Exercise and entertainment included the Bude & North Cornwall Golf Club, lawn tennis on Summerleaze with a croquet tournament in August, and Bude Cricket Club. There was also sea bathing, restricted by canal by-laws which had ordained years before that 'persons bathing naked in the harbour' should pay £5.0.0. The sexes were carefully segregated. The ladies had their beach at Crooklets while the gentlemen were left to take the plunge into Sir Thomas's Pit at the end of the breakwater. You could take Brendon's Day Excursions by horse-coach or charabanc to Boscastle for 3s 6d or to Widemouth Bay and back for 1s. In the evening there might be Mr Alfred Capper appearing in the parish hall in his 'drawing room entertainment as given at Windsor Castle and Marlborough House by command of the King and Queen'. On Sunday, to quote the *Directory* 'there was a large and fashionable congregation at St Michael's Church' with good singing under the organist, Mr Andrews. In the afternoon, with a very low tide, 'many took a promenade' and were entertained by a 'London artiste who built curious castles and made numerous amusing and clever designs'. Bath chairs could be hired from T. W. Maynard in Queen Street; Edward and Sons of Morwenna Terrace provided landaus, Victoria Midge Waggonettes, dog carts, jingles, charabancs and even a glass hearse with or without mourning coaches. The Bude Sanitary Steam Laundry carried out first class work, with open air drying, at the shortest possible notice.

In this period before World War I, Bude expanded gently as the relative importance of Stratton declined. A new water supply was developed from Tamar Lake, the old canal reservoir, and triumphantly turned on by General Buller under a banner proclaiming 'Success to our West Country Health Resort'. Six years later a new sewage scheme was completed, terminating under Compass Point. The Bude Electricity and Gas Companies provided light and heat from their own works.

The Edwardian season continued to flourish in Bude right up to World War I. No one would pretend that Bude was in the front line, but it played its part nevertheless. Horses were supplied to the forces as well as many volunteers from all over the neighbourhood. The 2nd Battallion of the DCLI was trained in the Drill Hall, formerly the United Free Methodist Chapel. A Girls Patriotic Club was started in Grenville Terrace, its varied programme including French and music lessons, with walks and games on the cliffs and beach, sewing parties, singing competitions and drilling. On the once weekly open day, members were encouraged to bring along a soldier, whether convalescent or not. There was a convalescent home on

Summerleaze Crescent, and many soldiers were nursed back to health in the bracing air.

There was always some danger of submarine attacks in Bude Bay, where the locally owned ketch *Kindly Light* was sunk. To guard against this menace an airship and anti-submarine patrol was organised from a base near Marhamchurch. But war notwithstanding, holiday seasons came and went; and the *Bude Guide*, which first appeared in 1909, was published regularly.

Two distinguished local characters, Sir Goldsworthy Gurney and the Reverend Stephen Hawker, epitomized the century in which they lived.

Gurney was born near Padstow in 1793 and educated at Truro where he was influenced by Richard Trevithick, the Cornish engineer. He first trained as a doctor and married, at the age of 21, Elizabeth Symons of Launcells by whom he had a daughter, Anna Jane, and a son. Moving to London, and while still practising medicine, he received a Gold Medal from the Royal Society of Arts for his oxy-hydrogen blowpipe. He then designed and patented (1825) 'an apparatus for propelling carriages on common roads and railways'; and four years later his steam-coach ran successfully from London to Bath and back. Flushed by success and anticipated wealth, he decided to build a country house near his wife's Cornish home and leasing from Sir Thomas Acland a sand-dune site at Bude, he built the castle.

Rival interests soon destroyed the financial viability of his steam-coach, so he switched his thoughts to lighting and heating. The Bude Light followed, using the principle of introducing oxygen into the interior of an ordinary flame. After trials in his own house at Bude, he took his invention to London where it was adopted for the House of Commons as was the Gurney Stove.

His wife did not enjoy life at the castle, so he sold the lease to Canon Maskell and bought Reeds at Poughill. Elizabeth died about this time, and some years later, when he was 60, Gurney married again. In his last years, and soon after being belatedly knighted, he was struck by a paralysis from which he never recovered. He was buried at Launcells; and his devoted daughter, who had looked after him at Reeds during his final illness, presented a clock to Poughill church as a memorial.

Hawker was born in Stratton in 1804 where his father was curate. During his lifetime he managed to be a poet, a mystic and a down-to-earth parish priest all at the same time. At the age of 19 he married the wealthy Charlotte L'Ans, aged 41, who was then living at Ebbingford. She paid his way through Oxford and became, and remained, the mainstay of his life for nearly 40 years, sharing the joys and tribulations of life at Morwenstowe where he had become vicar in 1834. Not long after Charlotte's death, he married his 'dear Pauline', Roman Catholic daughter of a Polish Count and governess to a family in the area. They had three daughters, and there is little doubt that she made him thoroughly happy in his old age. A few hours before he died, at the age of 71 in 1875, he was received into the Catholic Church. The conventional Victorian Anglican world was shocked and could hardly believe it, but he had probably been moving in that direction for some time.

Hawker wrote some superb poetry, but his fertile imagination was inclined to take control of his prose writing so that it is almost impossible to distinguish fact from fiction. He was essentially a humble man however, and over the door of the vicarage he built at Morwenstowe he had inscribed:

> 'A House, a Glebe, a Pound a Day
> A Pleasant Place to Watch and Pray
> Be True to Church—Be Kind to Poor
> O' Minister! For Evermore.'

What more fitting epitaph could there be?

LEFT: Parson Black of Launcells walking down Stratton Hill c1900. (AJ) RIGHT: Old cottages in Gibraltar Square, Old Stratton. (AJ)

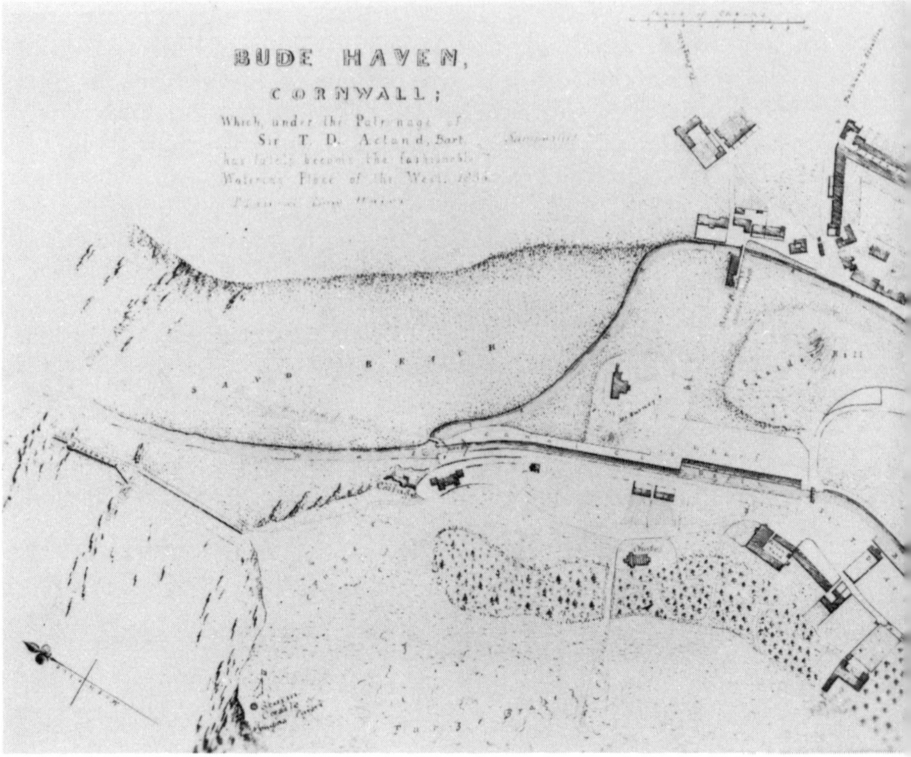

BUDE HAVEN,
CORNWALL;
Which, under the Patronage of
Sir T. D. Acland, Bart.
has lately become the fashionable
Watering Place of the West. 1836.

BATHERS

WILL BE ALLOWED TO USE THE

NEW BATH POOL,

at the end of the Breakwater, while Canvass is set up for Shelter, on paying **2d.** *each time for attendance, to the man in charge of the Pool.*

Canvass will be set (weather permitting) half an hour before half ebb Tide, and be kept up as may be found convenient and desirable until about half an hour after half flood Tide.

By consent of the Bude Harbour and Canal Company, and of the Lord of the Manor of Efford.

For further Information apply to Mr. GEORGE HEARD, Post Office, Bude Haven.

BUDE HAVEN, 1859.

OPPOSITE ABOVE: A map of Bude Haven in 1836, the 'Watering Place of the West' and BELOW: a 19th century engraving of the Strand at Bude, c1850. ABOVE: Expensive bathing in 1859. (RST) BELOW: Sir Thomas's Pit at the end of the breakwater, the new 'Bath Pool' of 1859. (MM) INSET: The Bullers Arms, Marhamchurch c1900. Now a fine modern hotel. (RST)

ABOVE: The Strand at Bude c1880. BELOW: Hartland Terrace and Othello Terrace seen from across Belle Vue, c1880. (RST)

ABOVE: The River Neet and the Strand c1880. BELOW: A print showing Nanny Moore's Bridge and Leven Cottages.

ABOVE: The Bude Hotel where Lloyd's Bank now stands, opened in the 18th century. CENTRE: Coaches outside the Falcon Hotel c1890. (MM) BELOW: The same hotel after extension. (RST)

ABOVE: Arches celebrating the opening of the Railway in 1898. (RT) INSET: Cutting the first sod of the Bude Railway in 1890. BELOW: A train in Bude Station, c1900.

ABOVE: A horse 'bus outside the station. (BSHFE) LEFT: Sir Goldsworthy Gurney, and RIGHT: Arthur Mills, son-in-law of Sir Thomas Acland and a pillar of 19th century Bude.

ABOVE: Croquet on the lawn of Gurney's castle c1890.
(MS) CENTRE: Gurney's Steam Coach in 1829. BELOW:
Spencer Howlett unveiling the plaque to Gurney outside the
castle, presented by the Old Cornwall Society. (MM)

95

LEFT: A photograph of Robert Stephen Hawker c1870.
RIGHT: A sketch of Hawker made by the Earl of Carlisle in
1863. BELOW: The hotel which Bude escaped; the Granville,
designed in 1899 for Summerleaze Down but never built.

The Kingdom Grows

For many centuries the church of St Andrew served the religious needs of the whole of what has now become the parishes of Bude and Stratton, with separate churches in the adjacent parishes of Poughill, Launcells, Marhamchurch and Poundstock. There were also two mediaeval chapels in the Bude area, one on Chapel Rock off Compass Point, dedicated to St Michael; the other dedicated to St Leonard. There is uncertainty as to the position of the latter. A sketch, made by Sir Thomas Acland c1825, shows a small chapel on part of the cliff near Efford Head which has since fallen away. This could have been the chapel of St Leonard. In 1934 however, the Rev F. C. C. Atkin, vicar of Bude Haven, claimed that the chapel had been attached to the then vicarage (Ebbingford Manor). He based his claim upon a vision which had caused him to convert an old Tudor passage into a chapel which was duly consecrated by the Bishop of Truro and dedicated to St Leonard. At the time, nothing was known of Sir Thomas's sketch. Old records show that there had been a domestic chapel at Ebbingford as early as 1413, though its exact whereabouts has never been discovered. It would have been normal for a house of the standing of Ebbingford to have included a chapel, and there is no reason why both chapels should not have existed.

In more modern times, Bude nearly did achieve a church dedicated to St Leonard. In 1908, Rev Frederick Wiltshire agitated for the building of 'a church of greater beauty' than St Michael's, and this was to have been dedicated to the saint. A site at the top of Belle Vue was provided by Thynne Estates, and for years a notice stood there announcing that a new Church of St Leonard would be built. Contributions were invited but nothing was achieved; the site was used for the post office in the late 1920s.

As Bude was enlarged following the construction of the canal, a need began to be felt for a place of worship additional to the Stratton church. In 1835, with this in mind, Sir Thomas Acland built a chapel-of-ease on his land above the canal—the starting point of the present parish church of St Michael and All Angels. At first, it was served from Stratton where John Skinner King was vicar. He was inclined to be late for his services, and it used to be said that while to most people the bells rang 'Ding Dong, Ding Dong', to the hurrying vicar they said: 'King come, King come'.

In 1848, the chapel-of-ease became the parish church of Bude Haven, a new parish independent of Stratton. Sir Thomas endowed the living, appointed the first vicar, Rev J. S. Avery and gave Ebbingford as a vicarage. The church was enlarged in 1876 and in its centenary year, 1935, Rev Cuthbert Atkin carried out extensive restoration which included provision of a massive reredos and extensive carved panelling which was executed by a local craftsman, 'Chips' Petvin, to designs by Macdonald Gill.

St Michaels did not fulfil all the religious needs of the people of Bude. There was, during the 19th century, a strong growth of Wesleyan Methodism. The first meetings held in Bude in 1820 were in part of the building which later became the vicarage. Next an old dwelling house at the back of Lansdown Hill was used and in 1835 a second Methodist chapel was erected near the Villa, now known as Villa Hall and used as a sale room. Sir Thomas Acland, the 11th Baronet, provided sites near Shalder Hills for two further Methodist chapels: one for a Free Methodist Chapel in 1879, the other for a Wesleyan Chapel in 1880. The former was abandoned in 1905 when the congregation moved to Flexbury; the latter became the Central Methodist Chapel.

The first Methodist home in Stratton was Molly Short's cottage, close to Town Bridge on Hospital Road. Larger premises were soon needed but were not easy to find as 19th century landowners were generally hostile to Methodism. However, one Billy Hayman bought two houses in Fore Street which he converted into a chapel but such was the public outcry that he was taken to court for violation of the property deed. He won his case but had to pay five shillings costs. This was awkward as he had no money. In the confusion of the moment, however, he put his hand in his pocket and found there five shillings exactly; how the money got there he never discovered. The chapel was opened in 1805. Thirty years later a larger one was built in Maiden Street on the north side of Market House; and Hayman, who had become a minister, often preached there. The present Methodist Church was built in 1890. There were also two United Methodist Chapels, one of which was opened in 1839 and is still in use.

During the present century, the Aclands granted sites in Bude

for St Martin's United Reform Church (formerly
Congregationalist) in Killerton Road and for the Roman Catholic
Church of St Peter in Bencoolen Road nearby. The pattern of
church development in Bude and Stratton was complete. The
parish hall was first built as a mission room at the end of the 19th
century, which explains its position in the centre of the town, well
away from St Michael's Church. As a mission hall, it was never
much of a success so its function was changed; a reading room,
now the British Legion Hall, was added later.

Today the church life of the area is full and congregations
which 50 years ago would hardly speak to each other in the street
now occasionally come together for joint worship and shared
pulpits.

ABOVE: A sketch by Sir Thomas Acland, looking north
across Compass Point from near Efford Head. The small
chapel in the foreground may be the ancient chapel of St
Leonard. BELOW: Outside Stratton church and cottages in
the 19th century. (AJ)

ABOVE: The Central Methodist Chapel at Bude. BELOW:
Interior of Kilkhampton church.

Guests and Guns

If anything conjures up a picture of Bude between the two world
wars it is the Atlantic Coast Express. You bought a ticket at
Waterloo, walked the whole length of the long platform to the
Bude carriages 'right up front'; name boards in gold lettering
proudly proclaimed the train's august title. This splendid train
left Waterloo at 11.00 am every morning with a through coach to
Bude. It arrived some 5½ hours later after numerous bangs and
bumps caused by frequent uncouplings.

Shortly after the formation of the Southern Railway in 1923 (by
amalgamation of the old London & South Western with the South
Eastern & Chatham) it was decided that there should be a named
train to the West of England to compete with those on the rival
Great Western. So the Atlantic Coast Express was introduced to
Bude in 1926. A new type of engine, the King Arthur class, was
then developed and used to take the ACE as far as Exeter. More
elderly engines took over thereafter and pulled sections of the
train to Bude, Camelford, Tintagel and Padstow. King Arthur
class engines were named after the knights of the Round Table
and included that rare phenomenon, a female engine, the Queen
Guinèvere.

'You can have anything you want', wrote E. P. Leigh-Bennett
in *Devon and Cornwall Days*, a Southern Railway publication of the
1930s, 'except the "pier and bandstand" type of holiday'. Bude,
was a place of character with no resemblance to any other seaside
resort; one of those exciting terminus stations. There were
extremely good 'diggings' which Cornish women own and run with
marked efficiency and good humour. You sit on the best kind of
down turf to watch tennis on Summerleaze Down: 'massed white
movement against a background of pale blue sea and lemon sand'.

The town had emerged unscathed from World War I except in
terms of human casualties. The two large hotels, the Falcon and
the Grenville stayed open all the year. The former described itself
as 'a family hotel, nearest the sea' with free golf for visitors on
Maer Down, a course abandoned long since, and 'omnibus meets

all trains'. The Grenville trumpeted in reply: 'Largest and only modern equipped hotel fronting the Atlantic'. The other main hotel was the Norfolk, a temperance establishment offering bowling greens and croquet lawns. But as Bude gradually expanded in the 1920s and '30s, many private properties were converted into hotels. In 1932, the Keat family bought that bastion of Victorian Bude, Efford Down House, and ran it as a residential hotel 'in its own glorious gardens and woods' with special winter terms offered as well as hot and cold sea water baths. Hartland House, once the summer residence of the Frys of Bristol, was also converted into a hotel. The town abounds with similar conversions, among them the hotels along Summerleaze Crescent and Penarvour at Crooklets, once the home of Sir George Croydon MP. No new hotels were built between the wars.

The Bude and Stratton UDC actively promoted the growth of the town as a resort. Summerleaze Down was bought from Col G.A.C. Thynne in 1921, and in 1930 the open-air tidal swimming pool on Summerleaze beach was built at a cost of £4,500, Col Thynne contributing more than half. The UDC also secured the foreshore from the Duchy of Cornwall and gradually developed beach facilities including a beach café and a rather wild looking structure known as Beach Tea Rooms. Private enterprise catered for visitors in other ways including the Bude Haven Recreation Grounds—providing tennis, bowls and squash—opened in 1924 on reclaimed land between the castle and Nanny Moore's Bridge. Bude's first cinema was built in Burn View by Robert Booth in 1922—the first film is said to have been *The Ten Commandments* with a Mr Moffatt at the piano. W.V. Graver, a local estate agent, later bought the property, and his son Colin built the present picture house in the typical 'palatial' style of the period. It was opened on 23 July 1936 with *Soft Lights and Sweet Music,* with Ambrose and his orchestra. The Headland Pavilion was built as a 'dance café' behind Summerleaze Crescent despite considerable local protest. Nevertheless it was able to proclaim itself in the 1938 *Guide* as 'the best in Bude…motor coach tours catered for at the shortest notice…Put your catering in our hands and success is assured.' And the owners gained some deserved popularity by handing out free milk-shakes to the children at the time of the 1937 Coronation.

More refined tastes were catered for by Miss Nibloe's Violet Tea Rooms in Belle Vue where you could enjoy 'dainty light luncheons and teas.' Pelvin Brothers and Edward & Sons, with their Morwenna Grey charabancs, offered daily trips to Clovelly, Tintagel and Newquay while from Samuel Edwards' Flexbury Garage laudalette touring cars could be hired. Also in the 1930s, Southern National took over the Strand Garage, now Julia's Place, and operated many excursions and a daily service to and from London. There were riding stables in the middle of the town and always, of course, the sea. 'Bude, the elusive will o' the wisp Cornish town that breathes the breath of the open Atlantic has no rival,' wrote a visiting journalist in 1937.

The summer seasons seemed to come and go with certainty, the ACE arriving every afternoon and the *Ceres* or the *Traly* sailing in with coal from South Wales. There were rowing boats on the canal and cream teas to be had at Rodd's Bridge, lawn tennis championships on Summerleaze Down, the blessing of the sea at Chapel Rock in August, fêtes and revels and fairs on the wharf. How peaceful it all was, until war closed the season of 1939.

In 1938 the Ministry of Defence purchased Cleave Farm, above the Coombe Valley for use as an anti-aircraft practice range. The cliff-top site afforded an excellent field of fire; shipping kept well away from this part of the coast and the rail-head at Bude provided the communications necessary for supplies. The camp was constructed quickly and the first guns fired in the summer of 1939. To begin with an elderly biplane was used to tow the target which, on reaching an altitude of 8-10,000 feet was let out 4,000 feet behind the plane. Later on the Wallace biplane was replaced by a Henley Hawker bomber; and occasionally a radio-controlled Queen Bee biplane was used for target practice, the guns being told to aim 'off'. Permission was sometimes given to shoot it down.

Another method was to catapult from the cliffs a seaplane version of the target as this could be picked up later by lighters operating from Padstow or Appledore, a laborious process which could only be carried out in the calmest of seas. A later development was to recall the Queen Bee by wireless, and in this way the first operational all-radio landings in England were made at Cleave. It was a perilous business for those on the ground as the plane tended to be uncontrollable below 20 feet.

As the war progressed, Cleave grew in importance, and it is said that more gunners were trained there than at any other camp in England. The place remained in use as a practice camp for territorials until long after the war and is still owned by the Ministry of Defence as a Composite Signals Organizations Station with huge radar bowls looking up into the sky. Soon after

ABOVE: Bude fair day, 1904. (MM) BELOW: Gen Redvers Buller turns on Stratton water supply, May 1903. Dr Arthur King is next to him holding hat. (AJ) ABOVE RIGHT: Crooklets, ladies bathing beach, c1912. (RST) CENTRE: Coronation tea rooms, 1911, (RST) and BELOW: Frank Trewin's store in Kilkhampton. (MS)

CORONATION
TEA ROOMS.

WATCHMAKER
& JEWELLER
CYCLE & MOTOR
AGENT
F. TREWIN
GENERAL
IRONMONGER
STORES

the declaration several of Bude's hotels were commandeered for military use, though both the Grenville and the Falcon were spared to become informal extensions to the officers' mess. Apart from the constant troop trains and the presence of so many soldiers, the war at first seemed remote. Then, in May 1941, some bombs were dropped at Hollabury, and the glow in the sky could be seen to the south as Plymouth was bombed later that year. One Blenheim crashed into the sea a short distance from the bathing pool, and a Heinkel was shot down at Morwenstowe where the crew are buried in the churchyard.

In 1941 Clifton College was evacuated to Bude to escape the air-raids on Bristol. The school occupied the Westcliffe, Erdiston and Hartland Hotels, together with the Headland Pavilion, all of which were surrendered by the army. At first, the small cricket pavilion on Summerleaze Down was used as a chapel. Later St Olaf's Church at Poughill became the school chapel, a fact which is commemorated by a plaque: 'Clifton College given refuge at Bude from 1941 to 1945 after damage by air raids to its home leaves this record of its gratitude for Cornish hospitality and especially for the use of St Olaf's as the school chapel.' Twenty years later a granite commemorative memorial was placed on Summerleaze Down. Clifton was the largest single element in the population of Bude during those years and integrated well with the local community. The school band was lent to the town for the 'Wings for Victory' and 'Salute the Soldier' campaigns; concerts and plays were put on, and it is appropriate that the last public performance before the school left in 1945 was *The Messiah*.

Clifton College OTC also joined the 1st Cornwall Battalion of the Home Guard which, under the command of Col Thynne and proudly wearing Grenville shoulder flashes, was responsible for the defence of an area which stretched from Morwenstowe to Week St Mary. Then, in 1943, the Americans arrived in Bude, their Ranger units training for D-Day on Maer and Sandymouth cliffs. Field Artillery Group 190, under the Texan Colonel Jim Dan Hill, were stationed here and billetted all over the town. Their headquarters were at Ebbingford Manor, their howitzers fired out to sea from Efford Down, and the pot-holes their tracked vehicles caused in Church Path are with us still.

Just before D-Day two Liberty Ships collided in a fog, and for days afterwards the sea was a mass of crates. Peanuts, cigarettes, typewriters and rations all floated ashore to be safely 'gathered in'. Cruel Coppinger's ghost must surely have stirred.

Two local characters: LEFT: Thomas Yeo, the Bude and
Stratton Town Crier, (RST) and RIGHT: George Henry
Johnson, the bathing patrol. (RST) BELOW: The storm
tower on Compass Point. (MM)

107

ABOVE: Coronation Day at Bude 1911. (RST) CENTRE: The DCLI enters Bude. Across the river is the drill hall, formerly the Wesleyan Chapel. BELOW: Bude c1915; on the right is the Central Methodist Chapel. (RIC)

ABOVE: Convalescent soldiers take a drive round Bude
during the 1st World War. (BSHFE) BELOW: The Strand
at Bude in the 1920s. (RST)

Captain Carlton Blyth, Old Bill Bailey of Bude. (RST)

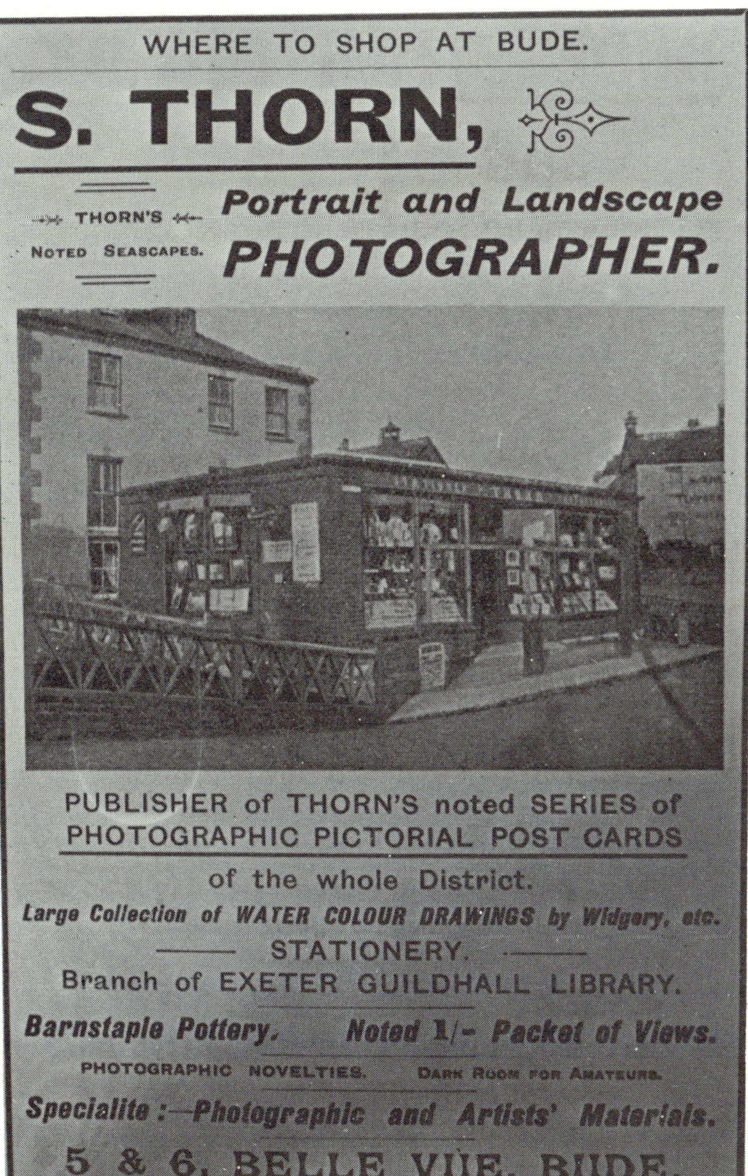

Spencer Thorn's advertisement, 1911. The source of many old Bude pictures. (RST)

LEFT: The doorway of Hazel Cottage, Breakwater Road.
RIGHT: A character of Georgian Bude. (RST) BELOW:
The recreation grounds opened in 1924. (RST)

ABOVE: The Summerleaze beach bathing pool, 1930.
(RST) CENTRE: The opening ceremony, 1930. (RST)
BELOW: Queen Street, Bude c1920; now one of the town's
main shopping streets. (RST)

ABOVE: Bude's first picture house, 1922. CENTRE: Grenville Terrace, with Hartland Terrace above, in the 1920s. BELOW: An aerial photograph of Bude. (MM)

114

In the Quiet Resort

Bude, and the whole of the Stratton Hundred, emerged unscathed from the war. *Tourist Guides* came out each year, the 1949 issue using the same cover picture as the one for 1938. There have been innovations since then as when, in 1973, the bikini-clad daughter of the town clerk decorated the cover and the slogan used was not only 'Come to Bude the Sun Does' but also 'Lowest Rainfall in Cornwall.' Both the girl and the second slogan caused a certain amount of controversy.

Soon after the war, the Chairman of the Bude-Stratton UDC ceremonially christened a new West Country class locomotive with the name of *Bude*. 'I pray,' he said, 'that a kind Providence may bring both the men on the footplate and those who follow as passengers to their destination safely and on time.' It did so for a few years but the railway was closed down by the Beeching axe in 1966, and Bude thereby lost a vital link with the rest of the country. All that now remains of the engine is the Bude coat of arms which had to be designed specially for it as previously the town had unofficially used those of Grenville. A design prepared by Major C.A.G. Chudleigh was adopted and it included the following main features: for the crest, a falcon standing on a gauntlet—well suited to the wild coast—distinguishable from the Acland crest by a background of the sun; a knight's helmet as is usual for corporations; two golden clarions on the upper part of the shield, the Arms of Grenville, with between them a silver cross from the Arms of Berkeley (the Royalist leader who became Lord Berkeley of Stratton); in the lower part of the shield a field of silver from the Arms of Blanchminster with two wavy lines from the Arms of the Earls of Stamford—together indicating the sun shining on the sea; surrounding the shield a black border of seven golden roundels from the family of Whalesborough and the Arms of Cornwall. Of the families concerned Acland is most closely associated with Bude, Berkeley with Stratton and Grenville with Poughill—the three wards of the town.

A different problem left by the closure of the railway was what to do with the old station site, which has been an issue of local controversy ever since. The main threat was a holiday camp for visitors which would have spread from the old station to the marshes. Nothing could do more to destroy the character of Bude. Local opposition has been strong and the prospect has receded, though the site has remained derelict. Meanwhile slates from the old buildings have helped to preserve the roof of Kilkhampton church.

Despite gloomy predictions that the loss of the railway would reduce the number of visitors, a matter of major importance to the town in trading and employment terms, this has not happened. Each season has been more successful than the last as more and more people find themselves able to afford a Cornish holiday and increasing numbers of overseas visitors come to Britain—a twinning union with the French town of Ergue Gaberic in Brittany, achieved in 1978, has stimulated this process. Car parks have had to be enlarged and a confusing one-way traffic system introduced.

Fashions in holidays are changing, with the emphasis on mobility and self-catering so that the demand is for chalet camps and caravan parks rather than hotels. Such developments pose a serious threat to the environment but provided they are neither too large, too numerous nor too obvious, need not be objectionable. This type of development has, on the whole, been remarkably restrained thanks to sensible planning and a concerned and watchful public. There have been some excesses on the fringes of the town and outside it. Penstowe, the Thynne home at Kilkhampton, is now a holiday village, though well secluded. This last remnant of the great Grenville estate was finally sold up after the death, at the age of 90 in 1961, of Mrs Thynne, so long a landmark in the area as she drove around in an ancient Rolls-Royce with a liveried chauffeur.

The year after the closure of the railway saw Westward Television nominating the 'surfing resort of Bude' as the best holiday value in Cornwall. Surfing on belly-boards was first practised at Bude, Widemouth and the smaller bays along the coast during the 1920s but in 1953 the Bude Surf Life Saving Club was formed along Australian lines, and Malibu boards appeared. The club was the first of its kind in England and the base upon which the Surf Life Saving Association of Great Britain was founded. It has gone from strength to strength, winning many prizes in national competitions. Specialist members train throughout the year, and it is a fine sight to see them in their wet-suits battling with the winter waves.

After withdrawal of the Bude lifeboat in the years between the wars, there was a long interval during which there were no formal life-saving arrangements, except for cliff rescue carried out by the honorary coastguard, George Bickle, and his helpers. But in 1966 the RNLI presented an inshore rescue boat which is housed above the lock-gates, so enabling launching to be achieved with the necessary speed. Augmented by the Royal Navy's marvellous helicopter service, volunteer surfers using kayaks and an Australian surfboat with four oars and a helmsman, the service is remarkably efficient.

Such activities are essentially adaptations of sport to a necessary and humane purpose. They have been followed by adventure training, mostly in relation to marine activities but also in elementary rock climbing. The hostile, sandstone rocks and cliffs present peculiar problems to the rock climber which could not be overcome until modern techniques had been developed. But now the face of Compass Point, in particular, has become a popular and extremely testing climbing ground suitable only for the expert. The traditional sports and games, except for golf and squash, have lagged behind these outdoor activities but cricket, tennis, bowls and both codes of football are played with enthusiasm if rather indifferent facilities. Squash, now that there are three courts, has become popular, due largely to the inspiration provided by Jonah Barrington, sometime British and World Champion, whose home is at Morwenstowe and who trained on the Bude courts.

While primary schools remain in the various towns and villages, Bude Grammar School and Stratton Secondary Modern have been combined into a new comprehensive, the Bude Haven School. This serves a wide area and encourages further links between Bude and Stratton. Several of the primary schools in the area have long histories behind them, having evolved from earlier foundations, notably at Stratton and Week St Mary. The Bude school was founded in the last century with an Anglican connection and the help of Sir Thomas Acland. In addition to these state schools there is St Petroc's in Ocean View Road, a preparatory school founded in 1912 and bearing a more than local reputation. Its pupils in their red caps and belted mackintoshes are a familiar sight as they walk on the downs or proceed in disciplined files to St Michael's Church.

'Sing me a song of a school by the sea.
On the Cornish coast where the wind blows free,
Where the breakers roll and the spume flakes fly,
Sing me St Petroc's, St Petroc's for aye!'

Bude Haven School shows signs of becoming something of a cultural centre for the area and is used for exhibitions, evening classes, concerts and for regular meetings of the Musical Society. When the Cornish Gorsedd, the traditional and ceremonial gathering of old Cornwall, took place in Bude in 1975, the concert was held at the school. This was the second Gorsedd in Bude, the first being in 1961. On both occasions the main events were on the castle lawns where visitors and residents alike were astonished by the sight of Cornish bards perambulating with solemn dignity in their strange blue habits.

There is also a flourishing North Cornwall Art Society, which annually holds a summer exhibition. Other such organizations prosper, notably the Bude and Stratton branch of the Old Cornwall Society which holds frequent meetings and makes occasional outings to places of historical interest. The Cornwall Naturalists' Trust guards the natural environment, arranges lectures and field outings and adds to knowledge of plant and animal life in co-operation with the Cornwall Bird Watching and Preservation Society. Rotary, Round Table, Lions Club, Inner Wheel and other organizations play their part in the life of the community. Women's Institutes, Young Farmers and the political parties are active throughout the area of the old Stratton Hundred. Numerous charities find willing helpers.

During the war, Dr Arthur King used to ride around his widespread practice on horse-back, much as his forbears must have done who had practised in Stratton for generations. Today there is a modern group practice under the NHS with an excellent and well placed surgery in the centre of Bude and the support of Stratton hospital. Distance from Plymouth and specialist services is part of the price residents pay for living in a remote and beautiful area.

Until the early 1970s local affairs were administered by the Bude-Stratton Urban District Council (responsible for the urban area) and the Stratton Rural District Council which looked after the various parishes of the Stratton Hundred as well as Poundstock. Headquarters of the UDC had been in the castle since 1947 when the building was purchased from the estate of the last private owner. The castle still provides an appropriate home for the Stratton magistrates, a bench whose history stretches back through the centuries, and the local branch of the County Library. The County Council administration has remained more or less intact but there were changes in 1974 with the re-organization of local government and the creation of District Councils. The theory was admirable (units large enough in human terms to support the cost of a full range of professional officers) but the area of North Cornwall District Council is enormous. It includes Launceston, Bodmin, Padstow, Wadebridge, Camelford and Bude-Stratton as well as the surrounding country areas with headquarters scattered amongst most of the towns involved. From Bude and Stratton, the administration inevitably seems remote, and considerable strain is placed on both officers and elected councillors.

The Bude-Stratton Town Council has a lower status than the old UDC and administers a minimum of services. But, with the parish councils in rural areas, it retains the vital function of keeping local government in touch with the people and making local opinions felt on a wide variety of subjects. This it does with considerable efficiency, in spite of a minimum staff. Town Councils are not empowered to run museums, hence the cumbersome title (Bude-Stratton Folk and Historical Exhibition) of the little town museum set up in what had once been a smithy, since extended, beside the Bude canal—an excellent example of local enterprise and local pride.

The surf boat. (MM)

The War Memorial o

120

...hurch in Old Stratton.

ABOVE: The bard's procession at the Cornish Gorsedd in
Bude in 1975. (MM) BELOW: The crags of Compass Point,
the expert's playground. (MM)

122

Fishing and pleasure boats at their moorings below the
breakwater. (MM)

ABOVE: The Bude-Stratton Historical and Folk Exhibition building beside the canal. (RB) LEFT: Jonah Barrington at the Bude Squash Courts. (MM) RIGHT: The Bude Coat of Arms. BELOW: The cliffs north of Bude; Earthquake and Maer Cliffs. (A sketch by Sir Thomas Acland.)

A Wealth of Wildlife

If you stand at the edge of the sea-lock, where the Bude Canal opens into the sea, you are quite likely to see the brilliant blue flash of a kingfisher as it dives into the water; and there may well be cormorants fishing nearby. There are always gulls on the beach—usually of more than one kind—and often small flocks of turnstones, little wading birds with red legs, either feeding below the slipway or flying through the spray. Should you then turn and walk up the canal you will pass above the estuary of the River Neet which is used as a feeding ground by a number of other birds, including duck and occasionally even a diver or a wild Brent goose. During the spring and autumn migrations various waders make use of this sheltered spot, with maybe a godwit or redshank among them. At low tide sea asters and bright green eel grass bring splashes of colour to the drabness of the stones. Across the river the relic sand-dunes, which were largely destroyed when the car park was built, still support some interesting plants including sea holly, sea rocket and wild mignonette.

Above Falcon Bridge, where the path runs between the canal and the river, there is a splendidly varied stretch of country and much to see. There are trees of several different kinds and widely different heights providing nesting and roosting places for numerous birds. There is the sluggish water of the canal, ideal for moorhens and little grebes, and the fast flowing river, meadows, reedbeds and marshland; a section of the latter has been declared a nature reserve by the District Council with a bird-hide provided in part by public subscription and in part by the government's imaginative Job Creation Scheme which has also carried out other useful tasks in Bude. Sedges and colourful flowers such as yellow flag, red campion, willowherb, meadowsweet and in places a riot of wild umbellifers line the canal verges and drainage channels. Butterflies, hawker dragonflies and bright blue damselflies are plentiful in the summer, while in winter the whole area becomes unusually exciting for birds. There are wading birds and wagtails and usually three or four stately herons. Goldfinches twitter as they clamber about busily in stubby willows bare of leaves. Blue tits follow each other through the bushes, snatching at insects as they go. Oystercatchers move inland from the coast and forage on the marshes where they may be joined by curlews, plovers and sometimes a flock of wigeon or some other wintering wildfowl. Secretive water rails flit their tails and vanish among the reeds and rushes.

In 1976 that rare and splendid fish-hawk, the osprey, spent several months in this locality, perching on telegraph wires and fencing posts and occasionally plunging into the water to catch a fish. It augmented this normal diet with rodents and carrion, and even swept down upon an astonished heron in the hope of making it disgorge a tasty morsel. Why this osprey should have broken off its migration to the tropics I do not know, though individual members of several species sometimes do this. It was mobbed unmercifully by the resident birds (notably gulls, crows and jackdaws) which did not take kindly to such a voracious intruder. Another unusual predatory visitor has been the marsh-haunting short-eared owl. Kestrels and buzzards are often in the area throughout the year.

At the other end of the town is Maer Lake, a damp hollow in a field partly surrounded by houses and liable to flooding after heavy rain. This pond—for it is little more, in spite of its name—attracts a surprising number of water-loving birds during the winter including some that are by no means common to the region: white-fronted geese, for example, and that strange dabbling duck, the shoveler, whose name derives from its enormous spatulate bill. Fortunately this field is a singularly unattractive building prospect, though speculators sometimes have different ideas.

Near Kilkhampton is Tamar Lake, an artificial stretch of water originally created in 1817 to supply the Bude canal. In 1951, after vigorous campaigning by local ornithologists, it was declared a Regional Wildfowl Refuge and Bird Sanctuary. Some 25 years later it was extended by a new reservoir immediately above the old which, thanks to the intrusion of modern filtration works and staff housing, has lost something of its almost primeval solitude. The particular importance of these two stretches of open water, together covering nearly 150 acres, is their situation on the western migration route of several species of both duck and wading birds, many of the former actually wintering on the lakes. Around the verges are mud-flats, marshy ground and open grassy meadows as well as reed-beds which provide shelter for the birds. Parts of the original Tamar Lake are fringed with trees where many species nest in summer and others roost throughout the year. There is also much of botanical interest with marsh marigolds and many other waterside plants as well as true water-weeds.

But birds remain the great attraction, and winter the most exciting season. Coots share the water with flocks of mallard and tufted duck. Wigeon fly from lake to reservoir and back again. There are teal, pochard, gadwall and usually shoveler and other less familiar species. Wild geese and wild swans sometimes appear. Herons, which nest about two miles away, often hunt in the shallows or perch on willows near the water. Curlew fly overhead, and snipe burst from the reeds where a bittern or even a night-heron may be skulking. Well over 100 species have been recorded. There are numerous insects and other animals among which is an unusual fresh water mollusc, the large pearl mussel, which can often be seen when the water level is low enough to expose the soft mud of the lake-bed. Tracks of both fox and otter have been noticed leading across the mud to freshly opened mussels on which they had evidently been feeding.

Otters have suffered greatly from disturbance and the pollution of rivers, and are now rare animals in Britain but still retain a seemingly secure foothold in this neighbourhood. Not only do these singularly beautiful creatures make use of Tamar Lake, they visit the canal occasionally and have been seen quite recently on the beach at Bude, not far from the lock-gates. Unfortunately the American mink, an attractive but villainous intruder, is a more common sight today. They take young ducklings and anything else they can find and also seem to be usurping some of the otter's traditional food supplies (eels, for example) so may have something to do with the latter's decline.

Other mammals are also numerous in the area where badgers frequent the wooded valleys and foxes abound—I have even seen a dog fox on the sands below Compass Point. Both stoat and weasel hunt among the furze and along the hedgerows; and most of the smaller British mammals are relatively plentiful, including the now sadly reduced little harvest mouse. Rabbits are making something of a come-back, red deer occur in large numbers in the woods near Week St Mary, and I once watched a hare swim the River Neet and then cross Summerleaze beach in hurrying strides. There are bats too. And one day my cat added to the list of local mammals by presenting me with a barbastelle, an uncommon bat with ears which almost meet across the top of the head and which had not been recorded in Cornwall for more than 100 years.

Marine mammals are not numerous in the immediate neighbourhood of Bude, though dolphins have beached themselves in Efford Ditch and the occasional whale (usually a pilot whale) gets washed ashore. Grey Atlantic seals breed in inaccessible caves below high cliffs near Boscastle and sometimes appear off the end of the breakwater or even further up the river. In the autumn, seal pups occasionally come ashore while still in their furry white baby-coats or at the stage when they are moulting. These rather pathetic little orphans, less than a month old, may have escaped from their mother's care or been swept out to sea from their breeding caves before learning how to fend for themselves.

In spite of this wealth of wildlife, it is the cliffs and the rocks which are the most noteworthy natural features of the region. The sheer, bare cliffs built up from alternate layers of shale and sandstone—the limit of the carboniferous Culm Measures of north Devon and north-east Cornwall—stand exposed to the constant battering of the waves, the wind and the rain. In some places the folding, faulting and thrusting of these layers have produced unique cliff and rock formations such as the great cascades of zigzag folds to be seen at Millook and other places along the coast. The most resistant sandstones form striking buttresses and slabs of rock some of which stand almost vertically upright as at Compass Point and near 'Earthquake', the scene of a devastating rockslide between Bude and Northcott Mouth. At the base of the cliffs, ribs of rock pitch both towards and against the ocean—synclines and anticlynes—while complex folding has produced such strange formations as the Whale's Back and Saddle Rock near the breakwater. Local stone of several different kinds went into the making of the breakwater, much of it being quarried nearby. Embedded in some of the sedimentary shales of these cliffs are hard, dark sandstone nodules which enclose the preserved remains of an unusual fossil fish, *Cornuboniscus budensis,* first found in the Bude Fish Bed immediately behind the swimming pool on Summerleaze beach. The discovery was made by Spencer Howlett in 1921 when he was still a pupil at St Petroc's preparatory school. Everywhere there are signs of natural weathering which is a never-ending process.

The elevated plateau of the hinterland is cut by short, steep-sided and deeply incised valleys some of which are truncated to produce waterfalls to the shore. These breaks in the cliffs mark the outlets of rivers, as at Bude itself, or of small streams. The result, as Charles Kingsley wrote in 1855 is; 'those delightful glens, which cut the high table-land, each opening through its gorge of down and rock towards the boundless ocean.... Each has its upright walls, inland of rich oak-wood and nearer the sea of dark green furze, then of smooth turf, then of weird back-cliffs which range out right and left far into the deep sea in castles, spires and wings of jagged ironstone.... such is the ''Mouth'' as these coves are called.'

The oak-woods remain in many of these valleys with their badgers, woodpeckers and butterflies such as the silver-washed fritillary. But much of Kingsley's smooth turf is now under cultivation or—since the reduction of rabbits by myxomatosis—has been overtaken by scrub. One result of this has been the disappearance of the large blue butterfly from its old haunts on the cliff-tops and in the valleys. This beautiful insect depends for its existence upon wild thyme, which grows particularly well on coastal grassland closely cropped by rabbits, and a certain species of ant with which it has developed a symbiotic relationship. Unfortunately these conditions seldom now obtain. But the downs and clifftops of this whole stretch of coast are well protected thanks to the foresight of the National Trust, the various local authorities and Sir Richard Acland who, as long ago as 1940, made sure that the fine Efford Downs should remain open space for ever.

In spring and early summer the cliff edges are lined with sea pinks. Pale blue vernal squills, wild violets, an abundance of lesser celandine and the occasional centaury bring colour to the grassland; the furze, with both common and western gorse, is bright with flowers throughout much of the year though sometimes it is covered by the red and tangled thread-like stems of the parasitical dodder. Mixed plant communities occupy the more sheltered spots with heather, hawthorn and blackberries as well as gorse. Small mammals make good use of the shelter these provide, as do farm animals in rough weather. Birds include stonechats, pipits and seasonally wheatears which flash their white tail coverts as they fly from one vantage point to another. Jackdaws, which have replaced Cornish choughs as the most common birds of the cliff-tops, wheel as they fly 'outlined in silhouette against the sky'. A kestrel hovers on almost motionless wings before it plunges down upon some hapless vole or shrew; buzzards soar, though not so frequently as they used to, for this fine bird of prey—a benefactor to man—is still persecuted by ignorant and mischievous people in spite of being protected by law. And the matchless peregrine falcon, which was brought near to extinction by the excessive use of pesticides, survives to make its eyries on one or two of the most fearsome and inaccessible cliffs in the neighbourhood.

On the steeper cliffs, where there is little soil, few plants are able to establish themselves. But the gentler slopes are swathed in scurvy grass, bird's foot trefoil and the yellow kidney vetch. Rock samphire, stonecrop, cliff spurrey and sea campion add to what is already a superb display with rock sea lavender closer to the sea. Gulls, ravens and fulmar petrels nest upon ledges on the cliff face, and a few small colonies of sand martins tunnel out their nesting holes in the softer soils of the cliffs. Rock pipits, oystercatchers, shags and cormorants are, after the gulls, the commonest birds of the shore. Orange lichens and green algae colour the rocks, and the charming golden samphire grows in surprisingly exposed positions.

Around Dizzard Point the cliffs are replaced by landslip scrub on which has grown up a strange 'surrealist' forest of stunted oaks some of which are so modified by the conditions that they grow to no more than six feet high. With mosses, lichens, ferns and unusual flowers the Dizzard forest suggests the sort of place that must have inspired some of Arthur Rackham's more extravagant fantasies. Almost equally remarkable is the buried, petrified forest which lies ten or twelve feet beneath the sands of Crooklets beach. It rarely shows itself and has not been exposed to view since 1932 when an unusual combination of tide and wind cleared away the covering sand.

Between the tide-lines the true seashore life takes over, a naturalist's paradise where a wide range of marine plants and animals are exposed to view or can be found by diligent searching. Worms, such as the curious but common tube worms, may be seen almost anywhere. There are rocks covered by edible mussels which are anchored to the surface and which, when covered by the tide, feed on plankton suspended in the water. There are many other molluscs, mostly single-shelled snail-like gastropods: whelks, limpets, periwinkles and barnacles. Seaweeds are of several different kinds each adapted to conditions on different zones, or levels, of the shore where they provide valuable cover for the small animals that also live there. The most common seaweeds are flat wrack, twisted wrack, bladder wrack and the thin textured laver, or sea-lettuce, a local delicacy.

The numerous rock pools introduce to the beaches yet another set of conditions so that the animals and plants which occupy them differ markedly from those of the open shore. There are sedentary animals such as sponges which are fixed to the rock surface and tiny free-swimming fish such as the Cornish sucker, with its false eye-spots, and the common blenny. There are shrimps and crabs with four pairs of walking legs, and beautifully coloured anemones. These often look like blobs of jelly when the tide is low but open up under water to reveal their petal-like tentacles. There are red and green algae around the sides of many of these pools and perhaps the red cockscomb seaweed as well as some of the smaller species of whelk and limpet. If you can then turn your eyes from these mysteries you will see the gulls circling overhead and maybe a gannet diving for fish in the open sea or a guillemot winging its way low over the water.

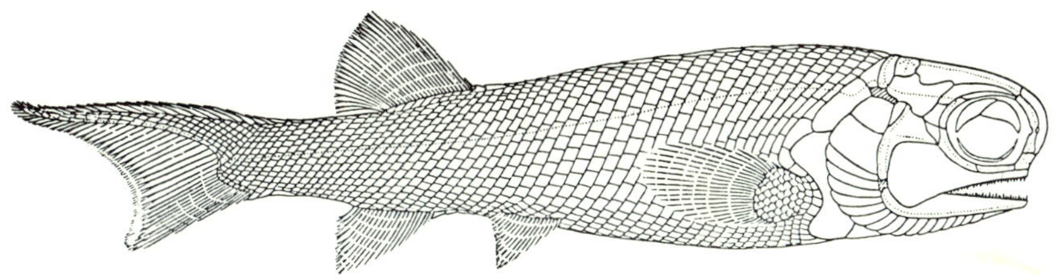

Reconstruction of the fossil fish, *Cornuboniscus budensis* which is preserved in sandstone nodules embedded in the slates of the Bude area cliffs. First found in the Bude fish bed near Summerleaze beach. (Z)

ABOVE: The Dizzard oak forest, looking north towards Widemouth Bay. (JB) BELOW: Vertical stratification of the cliffs north of Bude. (RB)

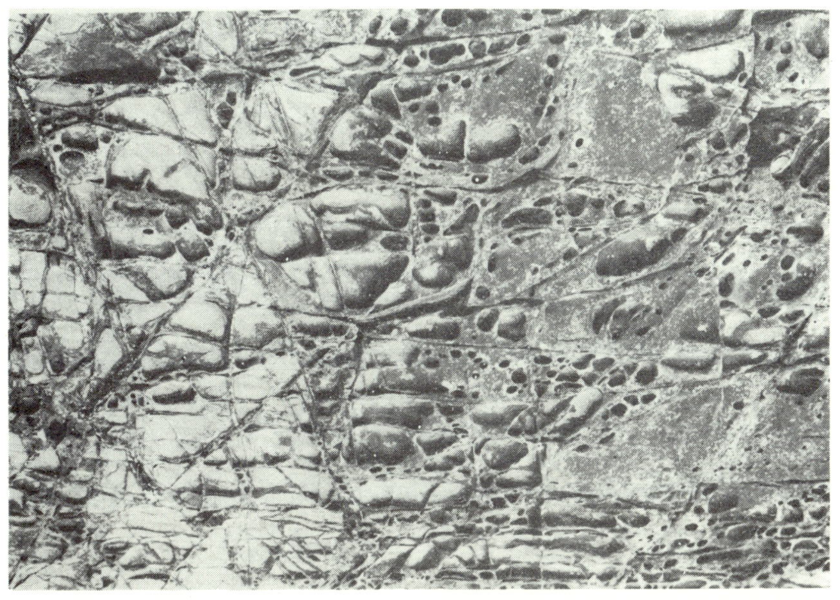

ABOVE: Honeycomb weathering of the sandstone. (RB)
LEFT: The prow of Compass Point: almost vertical slabs of
sandstone. (A sketch by Sir Thomas Acland.) RIGHT: Sea
holly and sea bindweed on the relic dunes of Summerleaze
beach. (RB)

Birds of the coast and canal; original drawing by Beryl McConville. From left to right. ABOVE: Heron, kingfisher, stonechat, CENTRE: Curlew, oystercatcher, cormorant. BELOW: Lapwings, mallards.

Plants of the coast
McConville. From
carrot, scurvy gra
Bird's foot trefoil,
Kidney v

Drawings by Beryl ... ABOVE: Wild ... squill. CENTRE: ... thrift. BELOW: ... samphire.

Index

Bibliography

Acland, Anne *A Devon Family* (1980)
Acland, J.E. *Bude Haven Links with the Past* (1912)
Arrowsmith, J.W. & Old Cliftonian Society *Clifton at Bude* (1945)
Atkin, F.C. Cuthbert *The Parish Church of St Michael and All Angels* (1935)
Balchin, W.G.V. *The Making of the English Landscape: Cornwall* (1954)
Baring Gould, S *The Vicar of Morwenstowe* (1899)
Baylay, Joyce *A Short History of the Church of St Andrew, Stratton* (1968)
Bere, Rennie *Bude Haven and the Stratton Hundred* (articles in Devon & Cornwall Post and Weekly News, 1962)
Bere, Rennie *The Story of Bude Haven* (1977)
Bere, Rennie *Wildlife in Cornwall* (1970)
Betjeman, John *Cornwall, A Shell Guide* (1964)
Borlase, William *Antiquities of Cornwall* (1754)
Borlase, William *Natural History of Cornwall*
Bray, John *An Account of Wrecks 1759-1830* (1975)
Brendon, Piers *Hawker of Morwenstowe* (1975)
Carew, Richard *The Survey of Cornwall* (1602)
Carter, Clive *Cornish Shipwrecks: the North Coast* (1970)
Chadwyck Healey, C.E.H. ed *Sir Ralph Hopton's Narrative of his Campaign in the West, 1642-1644* (1902)

Clarendon, Earl of *The History of the Great Rebellion* (1967)
Coate, Mary *Cornwall in the Great Civil War* (1933)
Crotton, C.P. *Bencoolen to Capricorno: A Record of Wrecks at Bude* (1902)
Darley, H.C. & Finn, R.W. *Domesday Geography of SW England* (1967)
Dew, R *History of the Church and Parish of Kilkhampton* (1928)
Dexter, T.F.G. *Cornish Names* (1926)
Elliott-Binns L.E. *Mediaeval Cornwall* (1955)
Goulding, R.W. *Records od Blanchminster's Charity* (1898)
Halliday, F.E. *A History of Cornwall* (1959)
Hamlyn, F.C. *Morwenstowe Since Stuart Times* (1930)
Harris, Helen & Ellis, Monica *The Bude Canal* (1972)
Harris, T.R. *Sir Goldsworthy Gurney 1793-1855* (1975)
Hawker, R.S. *Cornish Ballads and Other Poems* (ed Piers Brendon 1975)
Hawker, R.S. *Footprints of Former Men in Cornwall* (1870)
Henderson, C. *Essays in Cornish History* (1933)
Hoskins, W.G. *The Making of the English Landscape* (1954)
Kingsley, C. *Westward Ho!* (1855)
Lysons, D. & S. *Magna Britannia III: Cornwall* (1814)
Maskell, W. *Bude Haven—A Pen and Ink Sketch* (1863)
Nock, O.S. *Southern Steam* (1966)
Page, J.L.W. *The North Coast of Cornwall* (1897)
Paton, Jean *Wildflowers of Cornwall* (1968)
Penhallurick, R.D. *Birds of the Cornish Coast* (1969)
Penhallurick, R.D. *The Birds of Cornwall* (1978)
Pevsner, Nikolaus *The Buildings of England: Cornwall* (1951)
Polsue, Joseph *Lake's Parochial History of the County of Cornwall* (1867-73 republished in 1974)
Roche, T.W.E. *The Withered Arm—Reminiscences of the Southern Line West of Exeter* (1967)
Rowe, John *Cornwall in the Age of the Industrial Revolution* (1953)
Rowse, A.L. *Tudor Cornwall* (1941)
Slade, W.J. & Greenhill, Basil *West Country Coasting Ketches* (1974)
Thynne, A.G. *Sir Bevill* (1904)
Woolf, Charles *Archaeology of Cornwall* (1970)
Journals of the Royal Institute of Cornwall
Monographs on the Parish Churches of Poundstock, Morwenstowe and Kilkhampton
Old Cornwall, Journals of the Federation of Old Cornwall Societies
Universal British Directory (1791)

Key to Caption Credits

(A) J.E. Acland, (AJ) Andrew Jewell, (BM) Beryl McConville, (BSHFE) Bude-Stratton Historical & Folk Exhibition, (CW) Charles Woolf, (IP) Ivor Potter, (JB) John Beswick, (JH) John Hough, (JT) Major John Thynne, (MM) Mike Miller, (MS) Michael Smith, (PBT) J.G. Prideaux-Brune & Michael Trinick, (PC) Philip de Carteret, (PCMT) Philip de Carteret & Michael Trinick, (RB) Rennie Bere, (RST) R. Spencer Thorn, (RT) Roy Thorn, (SML) Science Museun London, (UE) University of Exeter, (Z) Zoology Society of London. Other illustrations are from the author's own collections. Sketches by Sir Thomas Acland (c1825) are by courtesy of Lady Acland.

Subscribers

Presentation Copies

1   **Bude-Stratton Town Council**
2   **Cornwall County Council**
3   **Bude Library**
4   **Sir Richard Acland, Bart**
5   **Spencer Howlett**

6 Rennie Bere	55 Roger J. C. Anthony	105 P. H. D. Kinsman
7 Bryan Dudley-Stamp	56 R. H. Troop	106 J. H. Sloman
8 Clive & Carolyn Birch	57 R. M. Bere	107 Mrs O. M. Ridgman
9 Philip Kerridge	58 A. Helliker	108 J. Ward(Crackington)
10 Peter Cloke	59 Peter Wonnacott	109 R. S. Pore
11 J. R. Alcock	60 M. J. Hardy	110 David C. Hockin
12 Dorothy I. Heard	61 Mrs D. A. Kingaby	111 Canon J. H. Adams
13 David Parsons	62 Miss C. Fallowfield	112 Diane Jean Andrew
14 D. L. Jury	63 Mrs C. V. Heard	113 Dr H. C. Gelard
15 W. E. Mackenzie	64 Adrian John Penfound	114 County Record Office
16 N. R. Rowe	65 Bennett	115 George Brendon
17 Mrs C. Blatchford	66 A. N. Benney	116 Mr&Mrs J. G. Oldham
18 Miss M. J. Venning	67 Mrs A. Thewlis	117 John D. Stanbra
19 C. R. Jewell	68 Mrs P. Holdcroft	118 Rev R.G.G. Hooper
20 Mrs Phyl Turner	69 D. J. Marshall	119 Mrs Margaret Budd
21 Rev S. W. Doran	70 Mrs Brenda Parsons	120 Wendy E. Pates
22 Mr & Mrs D. G. Spear	71 Mrs T. James	121 A. J. Tyler
23 F. L. Wheatley	72 Mrs E. E. Buse	122
24	73 H. N. Saunders	C. Seward
25 R. Bale	74 Dr K. B. Saunders	124
26 Mr&Mrs M. Saunders	75 Mrs Gwen M. Mill	125 Miss R. A. Sampson
27 Mrs E. E. Bass	76 Mrs M. Cooper	126 John Blowey
28 Roy Vickerstaff	77 P. Truscott	127 Andrew C. V. Hawke
29 K. D. Armstrong	78 L. B. Hancock	128 Miss J. A. M. Ball
30 M. L. Godwin	79 Mrs Joan Cook	129 C. A. Ball
31 K. V. Darracott	80 Mrs J. Eaton	130 F. R. Marsh
32 Mrs D. M. Larmour	81 Mrs J. Radford	131 Mrs J. Bell
33 Mrs J. M. Hicks	82 P.T. & K.M. Madden	132 E. R. Orchard
34 Roy Thorn	83 Graham Kingaby	133 William A. Brown
35 Mrs Hemmerle	84 A. Bruce Bartlett	134 Mrs D. B. Nourse
36 Peter Chard	85 Mrs F. V. Smith	135 Kivell & Sons
37 John Ball	86 A. B. Hubbard	136 Mrs J. M. Pearse
38 H. C. Thorn	87 Marjorie Taylor	137 B. R. Maggs
39 N. Duncan	88 R. W. Squire	138 Miss K. L. B. Price
40 H. A. Woolley	89 D. G. Fry	139 Carole V. Pedrick
41 G. Westlake	90 G. & A. North	140 N. P. Vanstone
42 David Wroe	91 Mr & Mrs A. Bowman	141 C. N. Cleave
43 Terry McGavl	92 John Harvey	142 Mr & Mrs E.E. Martin
44 Miss Jennifer Wade	93 R. Hunter	143 Mrs O. Martin
45 Mrs Christine Ogilvie	94 T. Rickard	144 Mr & Mrs R. Marston
46 Peter Mapleton	95 Mrs P. Leonard	145
47 Mrs Walter Lott	96 A. Walters	Mrs B. M. Currie
48 A. J. Celaschi	97 Michael Bennett	148
49 Mrs Pam Wade	98 V & A Museum	149 Vera Jennings
50 Mrs Rae Buckland	99 Terence Robert Heard	150 James E. Pritchard
51 John Stedwill	100 John Hooper	151 Lucinda Ponting
52 Andrew Jewell	101 S. F. Stannard	152 Michael Ponting
53 J. Thorn	102 E. R. Orchard	153 Mrs Vera Sanderson
54 Miss S. May	103 D. G. Orchard	154 Miss Ching
	104 W. H. Kinsman	155 Mrs B. L. House

143

156 R. Thorn
157 W. G. Rowland
158 Mrs Pamela Hands
159 Mrs Ciss Hands
160 Mrs R. E. Maude
161 E. J. Bell-Currie
162 R. C. M. Brewer
163 David Read
164 Exeter Central
165 Library
166 C. C. M. Knocker
167 J. M. Youle
168 Miss D. Tippett
169 William John Fearnley
170 Mrs E. M. Bailey
171 K. R. Matt
172 Mrs E. G. V. Kittow
173 Mrs M. K. Davies
174 K. D. Armstrong
175 William Thomas
176 Ward
177 R. C. M. Brewer
178 S. M. Wharpshire
179
180 Derek G. Reynolds
181 Mr & Mrs D. G. Spear
182 Paul Curtis
183 Owen May
184 Mrs A. R. Bloomer
185 Michael John Maine
186 G. & M. Newark
187 Roy R. Tolman
188 Mrs J. E. Shaw
189 Audrey E. Sim
190 J. D. Stratton
191 C. Harris
192 Mrs M. W. Wylder
193 A. Jolliffe
194 C. E. L. Trevelyan
195 Mary E. Williams
196 Col Gavin Young
197 Colin Metters
198 H. E. Redwood
199 John & Daphne Harper
200 H. N. Saunders
201
202 Mrs J. Gwynne
203 Keith J. Burrow
204 John K. Pollock
205 John S. Kinver
206 H. J. Kinver
207 Mrs C. E. Crouch
208 Leslie C. Symons
209 S. J. Record
210 Antony John Saltern
211 R. J. Beswetherick
212 Mrs M. Berridge
213 Mrs Diana B.
    Hall-Say

214 William Thomas
215 Ward
216 T. Parsons
217 J. A. Spiers
218 Arthur Venning
219 *Cornish & Devon Post*
220 L. H. Roberson
221 Budehaven School
222
223 Mrs Antoinette S. Cox
224 Cornwall County
258 Library
259 Mrs James Ellis
260 Miss Diana Ball
261 J.B. Pollock
262 John W. Eddy FRCS
    MRCOG
263 Andrew Garland
    Treseder
264 Brian R. Tuck
265 Mrs J.P. Winlove-
    Smith
266 Mr & Mrs R.S. Pope
267 Roger Venables
268 Mary E. Williams
269 Collin W. Brewer
270 Miss A. Compton
    Williams
271 Bruce Burley
272 I.A. Martin
273 John Blowey
274 Dr C.N. Wiblin
275 K.F. Baker
276 Plymouth Central
277 Library
278 P.G. Lobb JP,CC
279 Mrs M.G. Roach
280 Leonard H. Truran
281 County Record Office
282 F. Brian J. Coombes
283 Peter M. Dryden
284 Graham Facks-Martin
285 Justin Brooke
286 Mrs Betty Warden
287 R. Harris
288 John Richardson
289 Michael J. Maine
290 Sylvia Jenkins
291 C. Vickery
292 A.J. Theyers
293 David G. Bate
294 Mrs Grace Ridley
295 Miss G.E.
    Brocklebank
296 Sir James Smith's
    School
297 Rev Canon F.M.
    Smith
298 A.B. Bartlett

299 W.K. Colwill
302
303 Miss M. Flower
304
305 Dr J.M. Pencheon
306 D.G. Bate
307 B.T. Inch
308 Miss Morwenna Veal
309 J.T. Thynne
310 Mrs L. Roylane
311 Mrs J.R. Hunt
312 Miss M. Bradby
313 Malcolm Read
314 Mrs E. Squire
322 J. Clark
323 Miss J. Keeling
324 Ivor D. Potter
325 John S. Beswick
326 Miss M. Garland
327 Mrs J.M. Putter Gill
328 Miss Nicola I.A.
    Trzaska-Nartowski
329 Mr & Mrs A.
    Crossland
330 H. Stuart Young
331 Mrs S.E. Sweet
332 Douglas C. Davey
333 Mrs J.M. Jones
334 Walter Parnell
335 Mrs J. Gifford
336 Mr & Mrs Richard
    Clayton
337 Mr & Mrs L. Ladd
338 Miss M.E. Cobbledick
339 J.E. Gardiner
340 B.E. Carrick
341 J.H. Rickett
342 Mrs L. Greenwell
343 Lady Thompson
344 Mrs L.H. Gard
345 Mrs Mary Buhr
346 Mrs E. Hajee
347 F.R. Cann
348 Mrs Joan Smart
349 Gp Capt A.R. Wright
350 Mrs Joan Smart
351
352 D. Ridler
353 R.H. Jenkin
354 Mrs F.M. Fletcher
355 Rennie Bere
364
365 Crispin King
366 Bryan Dudley Stamp
370
371 K.F. White
372 Ian Martin
373 Bruce Burley
Remaining names unlisted

ENDPAPERS: John Norden's map of the Stratton
Hundred. (UE)

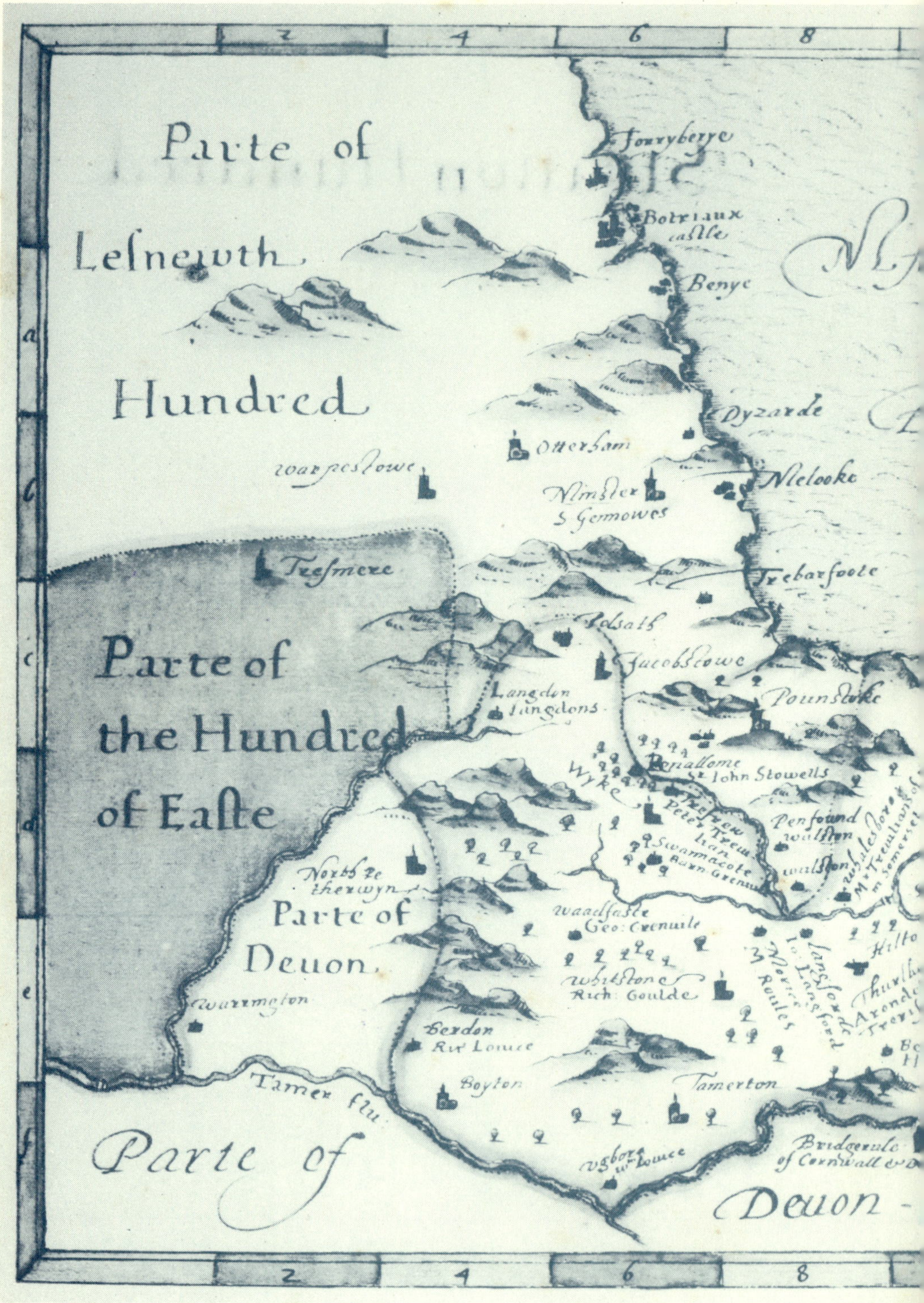

Parte of

Lesnewth

Hundred

Parte of
the Hundred
of Easte

warpestowe

Tresmere

Northpetherwyn

Parte of
Deuon

warrington

Tamer flu.

Parte of

fowryberye

Botriaux castle

Benye

Dyzarde

Otterham

Nimster
S Gemowes

Melooke

Trebarfoote

Tolsath

Jacobstowe

Langdon
Langdons

Wyke

Pounstoke

Trenallome
S John Stowells

Trew
Peter Trew
lian

Penfound
wallston

wallston

Penstoke

Swarmacote
Iuan Grenuil

M. Trewithanns
in Somersett

waadfaste
Geo: Crenuile

whitstone
Rich: Goulde

langsford
to Langsford
Mowris
Rualles

Hilto

Thurlb

Arond
Trevi

Berdon
Rit Louice

Boyton

Tamerton

B
H

vsborn
wt louice

Bridgerule
of Cornwall vo

Deuon